Do We Worship
The Same God?

MARK  DURIE

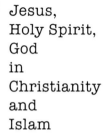

Jesus,
Holy Spirit,
God
in
Christianity
and
Islam

REVELATION?

GUIDANCE FOR THE PERPLEXED

CityHarvest
Publications

Commendations

Revelation? by Dr Mark Durie provides us with a succinct statement outlining the very significant differences between Allah and God. Dr Durie engages directly and graciously with the issues. He has supported his comments with quotations from the Bible, the Quran and the Hadiths, as well as from writers in the first few centuries AD. This book is easy to read and the points made are easy to digest.

Canon Dr David Claydon
*Former International Director of
the Lausanne Committee for World Evangelization.*

Revelation? is a timely book to wake people up to the fundamental differences between YHWH and Allah. Dr Mark Durie has approached this comparison in a scholarly fashion, basing his discussion on a wide variety of evidence. This, I believe, will make his book influential, challenging and a blessing to many who read it.

Dr Daniel Shayestah
Director of Exodus From Darkness.

This informative, incisive and much-needed book, *Revelation?*, fills a crucial gap: it clarifies a question that has been the subject of considerable confusion and obfuscation, leading to numerous wasted initiatives and blind alleys of all sorts. Mark Durie marshals the evidence impressively and explains it clearly, settling once and for all questions about the relationship between Islam and Christianity that have far-reaching theological, ecumenical and even political implications.

Robert Spencer
Author of The Politically Incorrect Guide to Islam (and the Crusades).

Revelation? by Dr Mark Durie includes copious references to the Islamic sacred texts and primary source material: Qur'an, Hadith and authoritative biography of Muhammad. It also draws on the author's detailed understanding of the Bible, Christian history and theology. Dr Durie combines within the study the rigour of the scholar and the commitment of the faithful Christian. The result is a work which provides clear guidance in an accessible manner on one of today's most frequently-asked questions. Those uncomfortable with Christian approaches to Islam based on robust apologetics will be challenged, but such approaches are needed in the contemporary world where many Muslims are levelling key challenges to the Church and the Christian faith.

Peter Riddell
PROFESSOR OF ISLAMIC STUDIES AND DIRECTOR OF THE CENTRE FOR ISLAMIC STUDIES AND MUSLIM-CHRISTIAN RELATIONS, LONDON SCHOOL OF THEOLOGY.

To make Islam more acceptable to enquirers and others, Muslims attempt to revise Judeo-Christian history and theology in part, by claiming that followers of these three religions worship the same God. Through a careful analysis of the texts, sacred to each respectively, Dr Mark Durie from his background in linguistics and theology, demonstrates that this claim is without substance. Allah of the Koran and the LORD God (YHWH) of the Bible are two distinct identities. This book is fundamental and necessary reading for all who search for truth and understanding.

Dr Stuart Robinson
AUTHOR OF AWARD-WINNING AND BEST SELLING BOOK, MOSQUES & MIRACLES.

Dr Durie has written a timely work: it does no favour and is no mark of respect to either Islam or Christianity to be fuzzy about their respective beliefs and values. Dr Durie carefully and astutely shows the fundamental differences between these two world religions in their beliefs about God, Jesus and the Holy Spirit. His research is based on the primary documents of both faiths. This is not a hearsay piece. The tone is fair-minded. An important work, culturally relevant and lucid in exposition. *Revelation?* is a must read!

Professor Graham Cole
Professor of Biblical and Systematic Theology
Trinity Evangelical Divinity School, Deerfield Illinois USA.

Dr Durie's primer, *Revelation?* - written in lucid prose - makes explicit the theological roots of Islamic supersuppressionism: in essence, the Muslim assertion that Islam as the 'primordial monotheism' represents both the 'true' Christianity and the 'true' Judaism. This concise text should be required reading for all Christians (and Jews) prior to engaging in interfaith dialogue with Muslims to avoid 'papering over' deep theological differences between Islam and both Judaism and Christianity, which undermine the very foundations of these latter two faiths. Christians will find particularly unsettling the Islamic conception of Isa - the Muslim Jesus - whose 'job description' includes the final destruction of Christianity.

Andrew Bostom MD
Author of The Legacy of Jihad:
Islamic Holy War and the Fate of non-Muslims.

Revelation? is stimulating, sensitive, scholarly, pastoral: just some of my responses to this excellent guide to the perplexed. Respect for the texts of Islam and Christianity form the basis of this insightful work. Mark Durie has set a high standard in interfaith engagement; brace yourself for the journey.

Bishop John Harrower
ANGLICAN BISHOP OF TASMANIA, AUSTRALIA.

Durie's book could not have been more timely. He analyses with great clarity and depth the fundamental principles of Islam and Christianity, offering a well-balanced analysis which acknowledges the important similarities of the two religions, without compromising on the hard issues. In this time of globalization, when the cultural jihad in the West is preventing the free expression of thought and belief, and is subvertng the whole ethical foundation of Judeo-Christianity, crucial challenges are emerging for the West's post-Christian societies. Durie's reflections provide essential and fundamental guidance which will enable Christians to engage in a dialogue based on truth.

Bat Ye'or
AUTHOR OF EURABIA: THE EURO-ARAB AXIS, THE DECLINE OF EASTERN CHRISTIANITY
UNDER ISLAM, ISLAM AND DHIMMITUDE, AND THE DHIMMI,

Published by CityHarvest Publications

PO Box 6462
Upper Mt Gravatt Australia

www.cityharvest.org.au
resources@cityharvest.org.au

Copyright © 2006 by Mark Durie

First printed 2006

Revised Edition 2007

ISBN 978-0-9775602-5-7

(Australian Edition ISBN 0-9577905-9-7)

Unless otherwise noted, scripture quotations are from the Holy Bible, New International Version. Copyright 1973, 1978, 1984, International Bible Society.

Printed in the United Kingdom and the United States of America.

Distributed in the USA and internationally by Ingram Book Group: orders@ingrambook.com

An earlier version of Part 1 was posted on the Answering Islam web site in 2002. This article has been plagiarised and re-posted on scores of websites since it first appeared. It was also included in Robert Spencer's 2005 edited collection *The myth of Islamic tolerance.* I would like to express my thanks to the many people who have given comments on earlier presentations of this material, particularly to Jochen Katz and Andrew Malone.

Cover Design by David Gray

Contents

Introduction

In these times many people are earnestly seeking an answer to this question:

In Islam and Christianity do we worship the same god?

The question may seem simple, but it is not. On the one hand Muslims will insist that we do worship the same god, and indeed the witness of the Quran demands that they believe this. On the other hand there are good reasons for Christians to challenge this opinion.

Here we will compare the LORD (YHWH) of the Bible with Allah of the Quran.

A careful study of the scriptures of Islam and Christianity shows that the LORD God of the Bible and Allah of the Quran are different in many respects. They have such different personalities, and different capacities, that they cannot be said to be the same. They can be said to have some attributes in common but in other ways they are so profoundly distinct that to claim they are the same god would only be misleading.

Rather than starting with the identity of God in general, I will begin with Jesus and the Holy Spirit. This is because God cannot be considered from a Christian point of view without reference to Christ, who is Immanuel – 'God with us' – and also the Holy Spirit. We will also take a close look at the identity of Isa, the Muslim Jesus, and the *Ruh Al-Qudus*, or 'holy spirit' of Islam.

A final chapter offers some practical advice to Christians and others who are seeking ways to apply this information.

What this book is not

This book is not meant as a defence of Christian beliefs or of the Bible, although some of the errors of the Quran are exposed in it. Neither is it a systematic explanation of how Islam works. It is focused very simply on the question of the identity of Jesus, the Holy Spirit, and God.

Transliteration of non-English words

Arabic words are given with a simplified transliteration in which the distinction between long and short vowels is not shown, and some consonant contrasts are not fully distinguished. The glottal consonants normally transcribed as ' or ' in Arabic, Hebrew and Aramaic are also omitted.

How should we refer to the Muslim scriptures? The older English spelling was *Koran*, but this has fallen out of fashion in favour of a more literal transcription. After all we live in an age when Peking is now Beijing. However because this really is an everyday word in the English language, I have simplified the transliteration from *Qur'an* to *Quran*.

References, verse numbering, names and dates

Numbered references are to the Bible and the Quran. For Muslims it is customary to give Quranic *suras* (chapters) with their Arabic names. However here the sura number is simply given, preceded by the letter Q for Quran.

Passages quoted from the Bible are from the New International Version translation, and those from the Quran are from Arberry's translation *The Koran Interpreted*.

Arberry gives numbers only for every fifth verse, and the references for the most part reflect this. In any case, anyone who wishes to look up a Quran reference must take notice of the fact that the numbering of Quranic verses is not standardized: one must always be prepared to search through nearby verses to find the right one.

There is one respect in which I have varied Arberry's translation, and that is that Quranic names have been restored, replacing the Biblical names used by Arberry. For example instead of *Aaron* I use the Islamic *Harun*, and instead of Arberry's *Gospel* I use the Islamic *Injil*. I have also retained the personal name of the God of Islam, *Allah*, in the translations. The reason for doing this is that biblicising these names in translation short-circuits the process of finding an answer to the very question of whether Jesus and Isa are the same, and whether Allah of the Quran and YHWH of the Bible are the same. Also I find it insulting to Islam to use Biblical versions of Quranic names. Another change made to Arberry is to use the usual *Hell* instead of *Gehenna*.

The Christian BC/AD year dating system is followed, rather than the Islamic one.

Difficulties in using the Quran

The coherence of the Quran has always been a matter of dispute. Is the Quran simply a 'very confused book' as the brilliant fifteenth-century polymath and theologian Nicholas of Cusa described it – whilst conceding the 'charm' of its style[1] – or does it reflect a unified, consistent world view and a coherent theological framework?

Arberry acknowledged the difficulty in using the Quran:

> The reader of the Koran ... is certain to be puzzled and dismayed by the apparently random nature of many of the Suras. This famous inconsequence has often been attributed to clumsy patchwork on the part of the first editors. I believe it to be rather of the very nature of the Book itself.[2]

The Quran, Arberry goes on to explain, must be studied and comprehended as a single whole – what he calls 'one message in eternity'.[3] Since the earliest years of Islam many Islamic scholars have overcome the difficulty of the lack of order within the Quran by committing the whole text to memory. That way, all its verses can be available simultaneously.

Like it or not, the themes of the Quran run through its chapters in a way which presents a maze for the unwary. Verses lifted from the Quran can be put to work to prove all sorts of spurious untruths and half-truths about Islam, and many people will depend upon someone more expert than themselves to help them navigate its shoals and deeps.

In Islamic tradition, interpretation of the Quran is a highly complex task, which requires an ability to link passages in the text to *asbab al-nuzul* 'occasions of revelation' in the life of Muhammad. Whilst the whole text of the

---

1   Hopkins, Nicholas of Cusa's *De Pace Fidei and Cribratio Alkorani*, p.971.

2   *The Koran Interpreted*, p. xi.

3   *The Koran Interpreted*, p. xi.

Quran is thought to be eternal and uncreated, it came to Muhammad in word-for-word increments over a period of several years. Each new delivery of revelation would relate to the immediate circumstances in which Muhammad found himself, so textual interpretation must proceed in the light of the context in which each passage was 'sent down'. It is necessary, in particular, to know the chronological sequence in which passages were revealed, as later passages may abrogate earlier ones. The sources of reference for this task of contextualising the Quran are the collections of traditions about Muhammad's life and teaching (*hadiths*) and biographies of his life (*sira* literature).

Establishing the time sequence of Quranic passages is no easy task, as the episodes of revelation are not in chronological order in the Quran, and there is often inadequate evidence to establish the context.

My personal view is that despite many internal inconsistencies – which will always give cause for debates – and the great difficulty of determining and sequencing the occasions of revelation with reliability, the individual verses of the Quran are embedded into a coherent religious world view and they can by and large be coordinated with progressions of events in the life of Muhammad.

In the light of this conviction, the reader can be assured that I have made every effort to give a balanced and true representation of the Quran's teachings – and of the Bible's also. In many cases I have offered multiple quotations from key passages, so that the reader can inspect the evidence for my claims for themselves. This is all the more important with a book as hard to use as the Quran. I also encourage readers to check what is said here for themselves. Despite all the inherent difficulties, the study of the Quran must and will be democratised. The subject is simply too important for it to be otherwise.

Final remarks and a dedication

The issue of the identity of 'god' in the Quran and the Bible is a profound and deep one. This small book by no means exhausts the possibilities for discussion! This is meant to offer guidance, not an encyclopaedic reference.

This book is dedicated to the Glory of God, Father, Son and Holy Spirit, for all eternity.

PART  ONE

Jesus or Isa?

In this section the reader is offered information and reflections on the 'Muslim Jesus', known as Isa, to help put the Islamic understanding of Christ in its proper context. This will lay a foundation to help us consider the identity of God himself.

Isa, the Muslim Jesus

Today we increasingly hear and read that Christianity and Islam 'share' Jesus, that he belongs to both religions. So also with Abraham: there is talk of the West's 'Abrahamic civilization' where once people spoke of 'Judeo-Christian civilization'. There has even been a proliferation of 'Abrahamic' conferences involving adherents of different faiths. This is new thinking which reflects the growing influence of Islam.

Islam sees itself as the primordial faith

> 'The word *Christian* is not a valid word, for there is no religion of Christianity according to Islam.'
> www.answering-christianity.com

It is fundamental to understand that the Quran does not regard Islam as a faith subsequent to Judaism and Christianity, but as the primordial religion, the original faith from which Judaism and Christianity are subsequent developments. Indeed these two faiths are regarded as secondary branches, developments which deviated from the trunk of Islam:

*No; Ibrahim [Abraham] in truth was not a Jew,
neither a Christian; but he was a Muslim and one
pure of faith [a monotheist] ... (Q3:60–64)*

So it is Muslims, and not Christians or Jews, who are the
true representatives of the faith of Abraham to the world
today:

*And they say, 'Be Jews or Christians and you shall
be guided.' Say thou: 'Nay, rather the creed of
Ibrahim, a man of pure faith; he was no idolater.'*
(Q2:125–129)

Another way of saying this, from an Islamic perspective,
is that the true 'faith of Abraham' was and is Islam,
and Christianity or Judaism could merit this name only
as a concession, because they derive their history in a
confused and corrupted way from Islamic roots.

The Biblical prophets were all Muslims

The Quran states that there have been many prophets of
Allah. Who were these previous prophets? According to
Q6:80–89 they include:

Quranic Prophet	Biblical Figure
Ibrahim	Abraham
Ishaq	Isaac
Yaqub	Jacob
Nuh	Noah
Dawud	David
Sulayman	Solomon
Ayyub	Job
Yusuf	Joseph
Musa	Moses
Harun	Aaron
Zakariyya	Zachariah

Yahya	*John (the Baptist)*
Isa	*Jesus*
Ilyas	*Elijah*
Ismail	*Ishmael*
Al-Yasa	*Elisha*
Yunus	*Jonah*
Lut	*Lot*

To this list of 'prophets' can also be added *Adam*, and some figures who have no clear equivalents in the Bible, including *Idris*, *Salih* and *Hud*.

According to the Quran these prophets all brought the one religion of Islam.

> *He has laid down for you as religion that he charged Nuh with, and that We have revealed to thee, and that We charged Ibrahim with, Musa and Isa: 'Scatter not regarding it.'* (Q42:10–14)

> *Say you 'We believe in Allah, and in that which has been sent down on us and sent down on Ibrahim, Ismail, Ishaq and Yaqub, and the Tribes, and that which was given to Musa and Isa and the Prophets, of their Lord; we make no division between any of them, and to Him we surrender. Whoso desires another religion than Islam, it shall not be accepted of him ...'* (Q2:75–79)

> *The Messenger believes in what was sent down to him from his Lord, and the believers; each one believes in Allah and His angels, and in His Books and His Messengers; we make no division between any one of His Messengers.* (Q2:285–289)

One of the most prominent of these Quranic 'messengers' is Isa, the Muslim Jesus, the last and greatest prophet before Muhammad.

There are two distinct primary sources for Islamic understandings of this Isa:

1. The Quran gives accounts of his life, and

2. The Hadith collections – recollections of Muhammad's words and deeds – establish his place in the Muslim understanding of the future.

We will consider these two sources in order: first the Quran, then the Hadiths. All this is reported with minimal critical comment: a Christian response comes in the next chapter.

Some Islamic beliefs about Jesus can seem quite strange to Christians, and inconsistent with the Gospels, but it is important to understand what the Quran says on its own terms, explaining its internal logical and consistency.

Isa was a prophet of Islam

Jesus' true name, according to the Quran, was *Isa*. His message was pure Islam, surrender to Allah (Q3:75–79). Muslims honour Isa, but do not regard him as the greatest prophet: this honour goes to Muhammad himself.

Like all other Muslim prophets before him, and Muhammad after him, Isa was a lawgiver, and Christians, as followers of Jesus, should obey him and submit to his law:

> [Isa speaks:] *'I will inform you too of what things you eat, and what you treasure up in your houses. Surely in that is a sign for you, if you are believers. Likewise confirming the truth of the Tawrah [Torah] that is before me, and to make lawful to you certain things that before were forbidden unto you. I have come to you with a sign from your Lord; so fear you Allah, and obey you me. Surely Allah is my sign and your Lord; so serve Him. This is a straight path'.* (Q3:40–44)

Isa's original disciples were also true Muslims ('submitters'), for they said:

> 'We believe; witness thou our submission [our 'Islam'].' (Q5:110–114; and also Q3:45–49)

The 'Books' and their people

According to the Quran, like other messengers of Islam before him, Isa received his revelation of Islam in the form of a book:

> Those are they to whom We gave the Book, the Judgement, the Prophethood... (Q6:85–89)

> [Isa speaks:] 'Allah has given me the Book, and made me a Prophet.' (Q19:30–34)

The *Tawrah* was Moses' book (Torah), and the *Zabur* was David's book (Psalms). Isa's book is known as the *Injil*, sometimes translated as 'gospel':

> And We sent, following their footsteps, Isa son of Maryam, confirming the Tawrah before him; and We gave to him the Injil, wherein is guidance and light, and confirming the Tawrah before it, as a guidance and an admonition unto the godfearing. So let the People of the Injil [Christians] judge according to what Allah has sent down therein. Whoever judges not according to what Allah has sent down – they are ungodly. (Q5:45–49)

It is because of these 'books' that Jews and Christians are known as 'People of the Book'. The teachings of Islam tend to treat Jews and Christians as a single category of people, so when the Quran speaks of 'People of the Book' this could refer to Jews, Christians or both.

It is essential to keep in mind that the one religion revealed in these books was Islam:

The true religion with Allah is Islam. Those who were given the Book were not at variance... (Q3:15–19)

As with previous prophets, Isa's revelation verified earlier prophetic revelations:

[Isa speaks:] 'I have come to you ... Likewise confirming the truth of the Tawrah'. (Q3:49; see also Q3:75–79)

...Isa son of Maryam said 'Children of Israel, I am indeed the Messenger of Allah to you, confirming the Tawrah that is before me...' (Q61:5–9)

Muhammad in his turn verified all previous revelations, including the revelations to Jews and Christians:

You who have been given the Book, believe in what We have sent down, confirming what is with you... (Q4:50)

This means that not only should Muslims believe in the Injil which the Quran says Isa received, but Christians ought to accept Muhammad's revelation as well:

Say you: 'We believe in Allah, and in that which has been sent down on us and sent down on Ibrahim, Ismail, Ishaq and Yaqub, and the Tribes, and that which was given to Musa and Isa, and the Prophets, of their Lord; we make no division between any of them, and to Him we surrender.' And if they believe in the like of that you believe in, then they are truly guided; but if they turn away [i.e. reject Muhammad], then they are clearly in schism... (Q2:130–135)

The corruption of the earlier Books

The Quran repeatedly says that Christians and Jews have corrupted and concealed the original form of their scriptures and done so at least partly deliberately:

*Allah took compact with the Children of Israel
… So for their breaking their compact We cursed
them and made their hearts hard, they perverting
words from their meanings; and they have
forgotten a portion of that they were reminded of
[i.e.* of the Tawrah]*; and thou wilt never cease to
light upon some act of treachery on their part…
And with those who say 'We are Christians' We took
compact; and they have forgotten a portion of that
they were reminded of. So We have stirred up among
them enmity and hatred, till the Day of Resurrection…
People of the Book, now there has come to you
Our Messenger, making clear to you many things
you have been concealing of the Book, and effacing
many things. There has come to you from Allah a
light, and a Book Manifest whereby Allah guides
whosoever follows His good pleasure in the ways of
peace.* (Q5:15–19)

*And there is a sect of them twist their tongues
with the Book, that you may suppose it part of the
Book, yet it is not part of the Book; and that say
'It is from Allah,' yet it is not from Allah, and they
speak falsehood against Allah, and that wittingly.*
(Q3:70–74)

*Are you then so eager that they should believe you,
seeing there is a party of them that heard Allah's
word, and then tampered with it, and that after they
had comprehended it, wittingly? … So woe to those
who write the Book with their hands, then say 'This
is from Allah,' that they may sell it for a little price…*
(Q2:70–74)

*Say: 'Who sent down the book that Musa brought
as a light and a guidance to men? You put it into
parchments, revealing them, and hiding much…'*
(Q6:90–94)

There is also the suggestion of concealing the words of God for financial gain:

> *And when Allah took compact with those who had been given the Book: 'You shall make it clear unto the people, and not conceal it.' But they rejected it behind their backs and sold it for a small price – how evil was that their selling!* (Q3:180–185)

Furthermore the Jews deliberately distort the meaning of what part of the scriptures they still retain, to lead Muslims astray:

> *Hast thou not regarded those who were given a share of the Book purchasing error, and desiring that you should also err from the way? Allah knows well your enemies... Some of the Jews pervert words from their meanings saying, 'We have heard and we disobey', and 'Hear, and be thou not given to hear', and 'Observe us,' twisting with their tongues and traducing [disparaging] their religion. ... Allah has cursed them for their unbelief, so they believe not except a few.* (Q4:45–49)

The Quran's claim is that Isa's Injil was lost in its original form – as with all the earlier 'Books'. It is for this reason, according to Sheikh 'Abd al-Wakil Durubi (b.1914), that Muslims do not believe in the Bible as held by Jews and Christians:

> The obligation of belief [in the 'Books'] applies to the original revelations, not the various scriptures in the hands of non-Muslims, which are textually corrupt in their present form.[4]

The mainstream Islamic view of the Bible is summarized on the website of the Islamic Affairs Department of the Saudi Embassy in Washington DC:

---

4   Keller (trans.), *The Reliance of the Traveller*, p 811.

The previous scriptures were meant for a limited period. Their use ended with the revelation of the Qur'an, which abrogated them and exposed their distortions and changes. That is why they were not protected from corruption. They underwent distortion, addition, and omission...[5]

Because Christianity is thought to be based upon a corruption of the Injil, it is a kind of debased derivative of Islam, but anything true in Christianity can be found in the Quran. The same applies to Judaism.

Today the Quran claims to be the only sure guide to Isa's teaching, so to be true followers of Isa, both Christians and Jews should 'revert' to their true religion by accepting the prophethood of Muhammad and following Islam.

The biography of Isa

According to the Quran, Isa was Al-Masih (the Messiah). He was supported or confirmed by the 'Holy Spirit' (Q2:80–84, Q5:105–109). He is also referred to as the 'Word of Allah' and a 'Spirit' from Allah (Q4:165–169).

Isa's mother Maryam was the daughter of Imran (Q3:30–34),[6] and the sister of Aaron and Moses (Q19:29). She was fostered by Zachariah (father of John the Baptist) (Q3:30–34).

While still a virgin Maryam gave birth to Isa:

> 'Lord,' said Maryam, 'how shall I have a son seeing no mortal has touched me?' 'Even so,' Allah said, 'Allah creates what He will.' (Q3:40–44; see also Q21:85–89)

This took place when Maryam was alone in a desolate place under a date palm tree (thus not in Bethlehem):

---

5   Al-'Uthaimin, *The Muslim's belief*, p.2, Chapter IV.

6   Compare with the Amram of Exodus 6:20. We will come back to this anachronism later.

So she conceived him, and withdrew with him to a distant place. And the birthpangs surprised her by the trunk of the palm-tree. She said 'Would I had died ere this, and become a thing forgotten!' (Q19:20–25)

Allah however had mercy on Maryam and provided dates from the palm above her for food and a stream nearby for drink (Q19:25–29).

Isa was a miracle-working figure. He spoke whilst still a baby in his cradle:

The Gospels testify to the crucifixion of Christ, but, as we have seen, the testimony of the Gospels is not accepted in Islam.

Maryam pointed to the child then; but they said, 'How shall we speak to one who is still in the cradle, a little child?' He [Isa] *said 'Lo, I am Allah's servant; Allah has given me the Book, and made me a Prophet. Blessed He has made me, wherever I may be; and He has enjoined me to pray, and to give the alms, so long as I live, and likewise to cherish my mother; He has not made me arrogant, unprosperous.'* (Q19:30–34; see also Q3:40–44, Q5:109)

Isa is said to have performed various other miracles, including breathing life into clay birds, healing the blind and lepers, and raising the dead (Q3:40–44, Q5:110–114). He also foretold the coming of Muhammad, referring to him by the name of *Ahmad:*

I am indeed the Messenger of Allah to you…giving good tidings of a messenger who shall come after me, whose name shall be Ahmad. (Q61:5–9)

Isa did not die on a cross

The Gospels testify to the crucifixion of Christ, but, as we have seen, the testimony of the Gospels is not accepted in Islam. According to the Quran, although Christians believe Isa died on a cross, and Jews claim they killed him, in reality he was not killed or crucified, and those who said he was crucified were lying: Isa did not die, but ascended to Allah. On the day of Resurrection Isa himself will be a witness against Jews and Christians for believing in his death:

> ...for their saying, 'We slew the Messiah, Isa son of Maryam, the Messenger of Allah' – yet they did not slay him, neither crucified him, only a likeness of that was shown to them. ... they slew him not of a certainty – no indeed; Allah raised him up to Him; Allah is All-mighty, All-wise. There is not one of the People of the Book but will assuredly believe in him before his death, and on the Resurrection Day he [Isa] will be a witness against them. (Q4:155–159)

It is a widely held view in Islam that to believe in the death of Jesus on the cross is to discredit his status as a prophet, for, as we shall see, the Quran teaches that those who follow Allah should experience success, and not degradation or humiliation.

Christians should accept Islam, and all true Christians will

With their corrupted books, Christians (and Jews) could not be freed from their ignorance until Muhammad came bringing the Quran as clear evidence

> The unbelievers of the People of the Book and the idolaters would never leave off, till the Clear Sign came to them, a messenger from Allah, reciting pages purified, therein true Books. (Q98:1–4)

Muhammad was Allah's gift to Christians to correct misunderstandings. They should accept him as Allah's final Messenger, and the Quran as the final revelation.

> You who have been given the Book, believe in what We have sent down [through Muhammad], confirming what is with you... (Q4:50–54)

> People of the Book, now there has come to you Our Messenger [Muhammad], making clear to you many things you have been concealing of the Book, and effacing many things. There has come to you from Allah a light, and a Book Manifest whereby Allah guides whosoever follows His good pleasure in the ways of peace, and brings them forth from the shadows into the light by His leave; and He guides them to a straight path. (Q5:15–19)

> Indeed, We sent Our messengers with the clear signs, and We sent down with them the Book and the Balance so that men might uphold justice. ... We sent ... Isa, son of Maryam, and gave him the Injil ... And monasticism they invented – we did not prescribe it for them ... O believers, fear Allah, and believe in His Messenger [Muhammad], and He will give you a twofold portion of His mercy, and He will appoint for you a light whereby you shall walk, and forgive you; Allah is All-forgiving, All-compassionate; (Q57:25–29)

Some Christians and Jews are faithful and believe truly (Q3:105–110), but any such believers will submit to Allah by accepting Muhammad as the prophet of Islam, i.e. they will become Muslims.

> And some there are of the People of the Book who believe in Allah, and what has been sent down unto you [Muhammad], and what has been sent down unto them, men humble to Allah... (Q3:195–199)

On the other hand, only anyone who shows love to Allah's and Muhammad's enemies could not be considered a true believer in Allah:

Thou shalt not find any people who believe in Allah and the Last Day who are loving to anyone who opposes Allah and His Messenger... (Q58:20–24)

This implies that anyone who opposes Muhammad is not a true Christian, nor a true Jew.

Christians who accept Islam or refuse it

Some Jews and Christians are true believers, accepting Islam: most are transgressors.

Had the People of the Book believed, it were better for them; some of them are believers, but the most of them are ungodly. (Q3:105–109)

Many Christian and Jewish religious leaders are greedy for wealth and prevent people from coming to Allah. They will be tortured in fires of hell for this by being branded with their wealth:

O believers, many of the rabbis and monks indeed consume the goods of the people in vanity and bar from Allah's way. Those who treasure up gold and silver, and do not expend them in the way of Allah – give them the good tidings of a painful chastisement, the day they shall be heated in the fire of Hell and therewith their foreheads and their sides and their backs shall be branded. (Q9:30–39)

Christians and Jews who disbelieve in Muhammad will in any case go to hell:

The unbelievers of the People of the Book and the idolaters shall be in the Fire of Hell, therein dwelling forever; those are the worst of creatures. (Q98:5)

Although Jews and pagans are said to have the greatest enmity against Muslims, it is the Christians who are 'nearest in love to the believers', i.e. to Muslims (Q5:85–89). Despite this statement, Muslims are repeatedly told not to take unbelievers, including Christians or Jews, for friends (Q2:25–29, 110–114, Q5:55–59, 60–64, Q9:20–24). They must fight against Christians and Jews who refuse Islam until they surrender, pay the *jizya* tribute willingly and are humiliated:

> Fight those who believe not in Allah and the Last Day and do not forbid what Allah and His Messenger have forbidden – such men as practise not the religion of truth, being of those who have been given the Book – until they pay the tribute [the *jizya* or poll-tax, explained later] out of hand and have been humbled. (Q9:29)

This verse, Q9:29, provides the theological foundation for warfare (*jihad*) against Christians as well as for the arrangements for non-Muslims to live under Islamic law after conquest. To this verse may be added hundreds of Quranic verses on the subject of jihad in the path of Allah against unbelievers — Jews, Christians and pagans — as well as many traditions about warfare found in the canonical hadith collections.

As just one example, the Quran claims that God has promised, not only through Muhammad, but also through Moses and through Christ, that those who die fighting in jihad against unbelievers will inherit paradise. In other words, both Christ and Moses are alleged to have taught the doctrine of jihad martyrdom:

> Allah has brought from the believers their selves and their possessions against the gift of Paradise; they fight in the way of Allah; they kill, and are killed; that is a promise binding upon Allah in the Tawrah, and

the Injil, and the Koran; and who fulfils his covenant truer than Allah? (Q9:110–114)

The ultimate goal of all this struggle is for Islam to predominate over all religions:

It is He who has sent His Messenger with the guidance and the religion of truth, that He may uplift it above every religion, though the unbelievers be averse. (Q9:30–34)

The Quran on Christian beliefs

Christians are repeatedly commanded not to believe that Isa is the son of God, and to reject the doctrines of the incarnation and the trinity:

People of the Book. Go not beyond the bounds in your religion, and say not as to Allah but the truth. The Messenger, Isa son of Maryam, was only the Messenger of Allah … So believe in Allah and His Messengers, and say not, 'Three.' Refrain; better is it for you. Allah is only One Allah. Glory be to Him – [far be it from him] that He should have a son! (Q4:165–169)

The Jews say, 'Ezra is the Son of Allah'; the Christians say, 'the Messiah is the Son of Allah.' That is the utterance of their mouths, conforming with the unbelievers before them. Allah assail them! (Q9:30–34)

Praise belongs to Allah who has sent down upon His servant the Book…to warn those who say, 'Allah has taken to himself a son'; they have no knowledge of it, they nor their fathers; a monstrous word it is, issuing out of their mouths; they say nothing but a lie. (Q18:1–4)

…He has not taken to Him a son, and He has no associate in the Kingdom. (Q25:1–4)

Isa was simply a created human being (Q3:50–54), and a slave of Allah (Q4:170–174).

The Quran implies that Christians believe in a family of gods – father god, mother Maryam and Isa the son – and they do this even though Isa himself rejected this 'trinity' (Q5:115–119).

The doctrine of the incarnation is disbelief and Isa announced that ultimate failure and a terrible doom awaits those who believe it:

> The traditional Muslim view is: that far from being crucified, Isa was taken up from the earth without dying.

They are unbelievers who say, 'Allah is the Messiah, Maryam's son.' For the Messiah said, 'Children of Israel, serve Allah, my Lord and your Lord. Verily whoso associates with Allah anything, Allah shall prohibit him entrance to Paradise, and his refuge shall be the Fire; and wrongdoers shall have no helpers.' (Q5:75–79)

They say, 'Allah has taken to Him a son.' … you have no authority for this. What, do you say concerning Allah that you know not? Say: 'Those who forge against Allah falsehood shall not prosper.' Some enjoyment in this world: then unto Us they shall return; then We shall let them taste the terrible chastisement, for that they were unbelievers. (Q10:66–74)

Isa in the Hadiths

Having examined what the Quran says about Isa, the Islamic Jesus, we now are ready to consider what Muhammad had to say in his own name about Jesus. These teachings are distributed among thousands of traditional sayings or *hadiths*, which were gathered together by Muslim scholars in the centuries after Muhammad.

Isa is the ultimate destroyer of Christianity

The traditional Muslim view is: that far from being crucified, Isa was taken up from the earth without dying. According to a saying of Muhammad reported by *Abu Dawud*, no further prophets will come to earth until Isa returns as:

> *...a man of medium height, reddish hair, wearing two light yellow garments, looking as if drops were falling down from his head though it will not be wet. He will fight the people for the cause of Islam. He will break the cross, kill swine, and abolish jizyah. Allah will perish [destroy] all religions except Islam. He will destroy the Antichrist and will live on the earth for forty years and then he will die.*[7]

What Muhammad is saying in this hadith is that Isa will return and will be the pre-eminent Islamic ruler in the end times, making war until he destroys all religions save Islam. The hadith then goes on to state that, after his return, Isa shall make an end of the Antichrist (*Dajjal*), an apocalyptic figure.

What do these sayings mean, and what is the significance of these references to the cross, swine (pigs) and the 'jizyah'?

- The cross is a symbol of Christianity. Breaking crosses means abolishing the Christian faith.

- In Islamic tradition pigs are also associated with Christians and are detested. Killing them is another way of speaking of the destruction of Christianity.

---

7   *Sunan Abu Dawud*, Book of Battles 37:4310; www.usc.edu/dept/MSA/ fundamentals/hadithsunnah/abudawud

- Under Islamic law the annual *jizya* tax is a kind of tribute or war-reparations which buys the protection and tolerance of the lives and property of the 'people of the Book', who are conquered non-Muslims living under Islamic law. As we have seen, the Quranic verse which refers to this arrangement is Q9:29.[8] The abolition of the *jizya* will mean there is to be no more tolerance or protection for non-Muslims. At this point the jihad will be restarted against all Christians (and Jews) living under Islam, who would then convert to Islam, or else be killed.

Another collection of hadiths known as the *Sahih Muslim* reports a variant of this tradition:

> The son of Mary [Maryam]...will soon descend among you as a just judge. He will...abolish Jizya, and the wealth will pour forth to such an extent that no one will accept it.[9]

To say that Isa will rule as a 'just judge' means he will rule by Islamic law:

> Since the Shari'ah of all the earlier prophets stands abrogated with the advent of Muhammad's apostlehood, Jesus will, therefore, judge according to the law of Islam.[10]

Moreover, after the jizya is abolished, an abundance of wealth will result, presumably from booty flowing to the Muslims from the conquest of all other religions.

So this is what the Muslim Isa will do when he returns in the last days: he will outlaw Christians and destroy Christianity, together with all other religions.

8   For further discussion of the significance of the jizya tax, see Bostom's *The legacy of jihad*, pp.127ff and Ibn Warraq's *What the Koran really says* (p.319ff).

9   *Sahih Muslim*, vol.1, p.287.

10   *Sahih Muslim*, vol.2, p.111, fn.288.

Muslim jurists confirm these interpretations: consider, for example, the ruling of the renowned jurist Ahmad ibn Naqib 'the Egyptian' (d.1368):

> ...the time and the place for [the poll tax] is before the final descent of Jesus (upon whom be peace). After his final coming, nothing but Islam will be accepted from them, for taking the poll tax is only effective until Jesus' descent (upon him and our Prophet be peace)...[11]

Ibn Naqib goes on to confirm that when Jesus returns, he will rule 'as a follower' of Muhammad, implementing Islamic (sharia) law.

---

11   Keller (trans.), *The Reliance of the Traveller*, p.603.

Is Quranic History Valid?

To this point I have presented teachings of the Quran as well as sayings attributed to Muhammad concerning Isa, the Islamic Jesus. I have tried to do this objectively, with minimal critical comment, so that the full picture of Isa's identity can seen in the light of the Quran and hadiths. Now however we will change gears, to ask whether there is any sense in which Islamic sources can be used as historical evidence for the life of Christ? The answer to this question is most emphatically, 'No, they cannot'.

The Islamic Isa is not an historical figure

The Quran's Isa is not an historical figure. His identity and role as a prophet of Islam is based solely on supposed revelations to Muhammad more than half a millennium after the Jesus of history lived and died. This makes the Quran valueless as a source of historical information on Jesus.

Jesus' name was never Isa

Jesus' mother tongue was Aramaic. In his own lifetime he was known as *Yeshua* in Aramaic. From this form of his name the Greek *Iesou*, pronounced "Yesoo", was derived.

This is like calling the same person *James* in English and *Jacques* in French, or *Karl* in German and *Charles* in English. The final *-s* in *Jesu-s*, the English spelling, reflects a Greek grammatical ending. English spelling follows the Greek, borrowed via Latin, because the New Testament was written in Greek, one of the widely used languages in Judea in the time of Christ.[12]

Yeshua is itself derived from the Hebrew *Yehoshua*, which means 'YHWH is salvation', and summarizes the whole message of the Bible. The name *Yehoshua* is also given in English as *Joshua*. So *Joshua, Yeshua, Jesu* and *Jesus* are all variants of the original name of Christ.

It is significant that Christ's name *Yehoshua* contains within it the Biblical name for God: the first syllable *Yeh-* is short for YHWH, 'the LORD', the personal name of God.

Even with all these variations, Yeshua of Nazareth was never called *Isa*, the name the Quran gives to him, and despite the efforts of many scholars, no-one quite knows where Muhammad got the name *Isa* from. It seems to be borrowed from the Greek *Iesous*, via another language, but it is hard to know where the ending *-a* comes from.

To this day, Arab-speaking Christians refer to Jesus as *Yasu* (from *Yeshua* borrowed via the Syriac), and not as *Isa*.

---

12   The letter *j* of English was developed from the letter *i* in the 1700s: the first King James' Version of 1611 wrote the name as *Iesus*.

Jesus received no 'book'

According to the Quran, the 'book' revealed to Isa was the *Injil*. The word *Injil* is apparently a corrupted form of the Greek *euangelion*, 'good news' or *gospel*, a term used in the Bible.

What was the *euangelion*? Was it a book as the Quran claims? No, not at all. The expression 'good news' was just the way Jesus referred to his message. This expression derives from references to 'good news' in Messianic passages found in the prophet Isaiah:

> *How beautiful on the mountains are the feet of those who bring* good news, *who proclaim peace, who bring good tidings, who proclaim salvation, who say to Zion, 'Your God reigns!'* (Isaiah 52:7)

> *The Spirit of the Sovereign YHWH is on me, because YHWH has anointed me to preach* good news *to the poor. He has sent me to bind up the broken hearted, to proclaim freedom for the captives and release from darkness for the prisoners, to proclaim the year of YHWH's favour...* (Isaiah 61:1–3)

The expression *euangelion* did not refer to a fixed revealed text, and there is absolutely no evidence that Jesus received from God a 'book' of revelation in the way Muhammad claimed to have received the Quran.

The 'Gospels' of the Bible are biographies

The term *euangelion* later came to be used as a title for the four biographies of Jesus attributed to Matthew, Mark, Luke and John. In what was a secondary development of meaning for the word *gospel*, these became known as the four 'Gospels'. Perhaps it was from this that Muhammad got his mistaken idea of the *Injil* being the name of the Christians' revealed book.

Most so-called prophets of Islam received no book

It is interesting that most of the so-called 'prophets' of Islam, whose names are taken from the Hebrew scriptures, received no 'book' or law code. For example, there is not a shred of evidence in the Biblical history of David that he received a book of laws for the Israelites. They already had the Torah of Moses to follow. So David was not a prophet in the Quran's sense of this word, and the Psalms (Zabur) are not a book revealing Islam through David, as the Quran claims, but a collection of songs of worship, only some of which are David's. Likewise most of the so-called prophets named by the Quran were neither lawgivers nor rulers.

> Biblical prophecy and Islamic prophecy are not the same thing.

Biblical prophecy and Islamic prophecy are not the same thing

The Biblical understanding of prophecy is quite different from Muhammad's. A Biblical prophecy is not regarded as a passage reproduced from a heavenly eternally pre-existent text, as the Quran is supposed by Muslims to be, but a message from God for a specific time and place. A Biblical prophet is someone to whom God reveals hidden things, and who then acts as God's verbal agent. Thus when a Samaritan woman called Jesus a 'prophet' (John 4:19), it was because he had spoken about hidden things in her life that he could only have known about from God. The New Testament does refer to Jesus as a prophet, but he brought no 'book': he himself was the living 'Word of God' (a title also used of Isa in the Quran, Q4:165–169).

The Bible consists of a wide variety of materials originally written for many different purposes, including letters, songs, love poetry, historical narratives, legal texts, and proverbial wisdom as well as actual prophetic passages. Despite their varied character, these are all regarded as inspired by God, yet much of this material was not actually written by what the Bible would call 'prophets'. At the same time, by no means all prophecies mentioned in the Bible became part of the Biblical text.

As prophetic history, the Quran contains many errors and anachronisms

The Quran's claim that Jesus was not executed by crucifixion is without any historical support. One of the things that all the early sources agree on is Jesus' crucifixion, as we shall see.

Other notable historical anomalies in the Quran:

- In the Quran Maryam (Mary) the mother of Isa (Jesus) is also reported to be the daughter of Imran and sister of Harun (Aaron) and Musa (Moses):

    When the wife of Imran said 'Lord, I have vowed to Thee in dedication, what is within my womb. Receive Thou this from me; Thou hearest and knowest.' And when she gave birth to her she said, 'Lord, I have given birth to her, a female … And I have named her Maryam… (Q3:32–33)

    Later, when Maryam has given birth to the child Isa out of wedlock, and people accuse her of impurity, she is addressed as the 'sister of Harun (Aaron)'.

> *"Maryam, thou has surely committed a monstrous thing! Sister of Harun, thy father was not a wicked man, nor was thy mother a woman unchaste."* (Q19:29)

It is made clear that this Harun is the brother of Musa (Moses):

> *And mention in the Book Musa; ... We gave him his brother Harun, of our mercy, a Prophet.* (Q19:52–54)

- The father of the Biblical Miriam at the time of the Exodus was indeed Amram (Exodus 6:20) and Miriam's brothers were Moses and Aaron. However the Quran confuses this Miriam with the New Testament's Mary (Hebrew *Miriam*) the mother of Jesus.[13] Muhammad was apparently under the impression that Moses was Jesus' uncle. The two Miriams shared a name, but they lived more than a thousand years apart!

- In this and other cases, the Quran conflates the timelines of the Bible. An obvious explanation is that Muhammad had heard of various fragments of stories from the Bible, and patched these together without understanding their place in the overall narrative of the Bible.

- In the Bible Haman is the minister of Ahasuerus in Media and Persia (Esther 3:1–2). Yet the Quran places him over a thousand years earlier, as a minister of Pharaoh in Egypt (Q28:5), thus mixing up the Exodus with the story of Esther.

- The Quran has a Samaritan making the golden calf, which was worshipped by the Israelites in the wilderness (Q20:85) during the Exodus. In fact

---

13   Although a hadith has Muhammad saying that Mary the mother of Jesus was not in fact the sister of Aaron and Moses (*Sahih Muslim*, vol.3, 5326), this must be regarded as a later invention to make up for the errors in the Quran.

it was Aaron who made the calf (Exodus 34:1–6). In any case, neither the Samaritans nor the place name Samaria came into existence until centuries later, when it was used to refer to the descendants of the northern Israelites.

- The implication that Christians believe in three gods – father, son Isa (Jesus) and mother Maryam (Mary) (Q5:115–119) – is mistaken. The Quran is also wrong to claim that Jews say Ezra was a son of God (Q9:30). This charge of polytheism against both Christianity and Judaism is ill-informed and false (Deuteronomy 6:4, James 2:19a).

- The story of the 'prophet' known as the 'two horned one' (Q18:82) is derived from the Romance of Alexander. However Alexander the Great was no Muslim!

- The problem of the name *Isa* has already been discussed. Other Biblical names are also misunderstood in the Quran, and their meanings lost. For example *Elisha*, which means 'God is salvation', is given in the Quran as *al-Yasa*, turning *El* ('God') into *al-* ('the'). Islamic tradition did the same to Alexander the Great, calling him *al-Iskandar* ('the Iskandar'). Abraham ('father of many', Genesis 17:5) might have been better represented as something like *Aburahim* ('father of mercy') instead of *Ibrahim*, which has no meaning in Arabic at all.

- The Quran has David making chain mail using iron rings. He was able do this because Allah made iron soft for him:

  > *And We gave Dawud bounty from Us: 'O you mountains, echo Allah's praises with him, and you birds!' And We softened for him iron: 'Fashion wide coats of mail, and*

measure well the links'. (Q34:10; see also Q21:80)

Yet David lived at the very beginning of the iron age (c.1000BC), when there were no blacksmiths in Israel (1 Samuel 13:19); David was a shepherd, not a blacksmith; and most important of all, chain mail was not to be invented for another 800 years! (Goliath's famous mail shirt was bronze scale armour: the Hebrew word in 1 Samuel 17:5 is the same as 'fish scale'.)

- The Old Testament, the Hebrew Bible, was the Bible of Jesus. It is inconsistent to maintain that Christ was a prophet, and at the same time to claim that the Jews had corrupted their scriptures, because it is inconceivable that Isa the prophet of Islam could have believed in and used a corrupted Bible. We can know with great certainty that Jesus' Bible is the same text relied upon by Jews to this very day. In truth Jesus was a witness to the enduring preservation of the Torah:

> *'I tell you the truth, until heaven and earth disappear, not the smallest letter, not the least stroke of a pen, will be any means disappear from the Law...'* (Matthew 5:18)

- The Quran displays little understanding of what is in the Bible and what is not. At one point a command is said to be 'prescribed for the Children of Israel' – implying it was from the Torah – but the reference is in fact to the Talmud:

> *Therefore we prescribed for the Children of Israel that whoso slays a soul not to retaliate for a soul slain, nor for corruption done in the land, shall be as if he had slain mankind altogether; and who gives life to*

a soul, shall be as if he had given life to mankind altogether. (Q5:35–39)

- Many Quranic stories can be traced to Jewish and Christian folktales and other apocryphal literature. For example a story of Abraham destroying idols (Q37:85–94) is from a legend reported in the Genesis Rabbah, a Jewish commentary compiled in the fourth or fifth century AD. The Quranic story of Zachariah, father of John the Baptist, is based upon a second-century Christian fable.

- The Quran claims that the gospel and the law of Moses both taught martyrdom in jihad, with a promise of paradise for those who die trying to kill the enemies of God (Q9:110–114). Nothing could be further from the truth. The Torah contains no such promise. Moreover, far from teaching paradise for those who fall in battle, Jesus himself forbad fighting for the faith, commanding his chief disciple Peter to 'put your sword away' (John 18:11), and warning his followers that 'all who draw the sword will die by the sword' (Matthew 26:52). He also informed Pilate that because his 'kingdom is not of this world' his followers did not fight to prevent his arrest (John 18:36). Finally, Jesus never instructed his followers to kill their enemies, but did command love for enemies (Matthew 5:43–45). If his disciples would only do this, Jesus said, they would be like God himself.

All these problems are further evidence that the Quran cannot be used as a source for the life of Christ. Virtually everything the Quran says about the life of Jesus which is not found in the Bible can be traced to fables composed more than a hundred years after Jesus' death. The story of Jesus being born under a palm tree is also based on a late fable, as is the story of Jesus making clay birds come to life.[14]

Jesus' title of *Messiah*, which the Quran uses, finds no explanation in the Quran, and Muslim scholars have never been able to reach a consensus on what it means. Yet in the Bible, from which it is so obviously taken, the concept of the Messiah, the 'anointed one', is plain, easy to understand, and is well integrated into a whole theological system, having a long prophetic history.

Jesus' alleged foretelling of Muhammad's coming (Q61:5–9) appears to be based on a garbled reading of John 14:26, a passage which in fact refers quite clearly to the Holy Spirit.

> The Biblical narratives are rich with historical details, many confirmed by archaeology.

When we examine the four Gospel accounts, we find that the Hebrew scriptures were Jesus' Bible. He affirmed their authority and reliability and preached from them, quoting them frequently. From these same scriptures he knew God as *Adonai Elohim*, the Lord God of Israel. Of course he did not call God *Allah*.

The Biblical narratives are rich with historical details, many confirmed by archaeology. They cover more than a thousand years, and reveal a long process of technological and cultural development. In contrast the Quran's sacred history is devoid of archaeological support. Its fragmentary and disjointed stories offer no authentic reflection of historical cultures. No place name from ancient Israel is mentioned, not even Jerusalem.

---

14   The story of Jesus bringing clay birds to life derives from the Infancy Gospel of Thomas, an apocryphal text with fantastic mythical stories, some of them malevolent, about the childhood of Jesus. Scholars date this text to the late second century AD.

Moreover, many of the supposed historical events reported in the Quran have no independent verification. For example we are told that Abraham and Ishmael built the Kaaba in Mecca (Q2:127), but this is totally without support. The Biblical account, more than a thousand years older, does not place Abraham anywhere near Mecca.

Conclusion: the Quran is not a credible source for Biblical history

The Quran, written in the seventh century AD, cannot be regarded as having any authority whatsoever to inform us about Jesus of Nazareth. It offers no valid evidence for its claims about Biblical history, and its numerous historical errors reflect a garbled understanding of Biblical history.

The True Jesus of Nazareth

In contrast to the Quran, the Bible is a genuine historical source for information on the life, teaching and actions of Jesus of Nazareth. As a source its core narrative is supported by non-Christian references to Jesus, both pagan and Jewish. Most of these make mention of his death by crucifixion:

- Tacitus (AD55–120), a renowned historian of ancient Rome, wrote in the first decades of the second century that:

  > *Christus...was put to death by Pontius Pilate, procurator of Judea in the reign of Tiberius: but the pernicious superstition, repressed for a time, broke out again, not only through Judea, where the mischief originated, but through the city of Rome also. (Annals 15:44)*

- Suetonius, writing around AD120, tells of disturbances of the Jews at the 'instigation of Chrestus', during the time of the emperor Claudius. This could refer to Jesus, and appears to relate to the events of Acts 18:2, which took place in AD49.

- Thallus, a secular historian writing perhaps around AD52 refers to the death of Jesus in a discussion of the darkness over the land after his death. The original is lost, but Thallus' arguments – explaining what happened as a solar eclipse – are referred to by Julius Africanus in the early third century.

- Mara Bar-Serapion, a Syrian writing after the destruction of the Temple in AD70, mentions the earlier execution of Jesus, whom he calls a 'King'.

- The Babylonian Talmud refers to the crucifixion (calling it a hanging) of Jesus the Nazarene on the eve of the Passover. In the Talmud Jesus is also called the illegitimate son of Mary.

- The Jewish historian Josephus describes Jesus' crucifixion under Pilate in his Antiquities, written about AD93/94. Josephus also refers to James the brother of Jesus and his execution during the time of Ananus (or Annas) the high priest (cf. Acts 12:2).

Paul's Epistles

Paul's epistles were written in the interval 20–30 years after Jesus' death. They are valuable historical documents, not least because they contain credal confessions which undoubtedly date to the first few decades of the Christian community.

Paul, formerly a fierce opponent of Christians, became a believer in Jesus within a few years of Jesus' crucifixion. He writes in his first letter to the Corinthians:

> *For what I received I passed on to you as of first importance: that Christ died for our sins according to the Scriptures, that he was buried, that he was raised on the third day according to the Scriptures,*

and that he appeared to Peter, and then to the Twelve. After that, he appeared to more than five hundred of the brothers at the same time, most of whom are still living, though some have fallen asleep. Then he appeared to James, then to all the apostles, and last of all he appeared to me also, as to one abnormally born. (1 Corinthians 15:3–8)

This makes clear that belief in the death of Jesus was present from the beginning of Christianity.

The four Gospels

The four Gospels were written down in the period 20–60 years after Jesus' death, within living memory of the events they describe.

The events which the Gospels describe for the most part took place in the full light of public scrutiny. Jesus' teaching was followed by large crowds. There were very many witnesses to the events of his life. His death was a public execution.

Manuscript evidence for the Bible and its transmission

The manuscript evidence for the Greek scriptures is overwhelming, far greater than for all other ancient texts. Thousands of manuscripts attest to them. Whilst there are copying

> The manuscript evidence for the Greek scriptures is overwhelming, far greater than for all other ancient texts.

errors, as might be expected from the hand of copyists, these are almost all comparatively minor and the basic integrity of the copying process is richly supported.

Furthermore, when Western Christians studied the Hebrew scriptures during the Renaissance, they found them to agree remarkably closely with their Greek and Latin translations which had themselves been copied again and again over a thousand years. There were copying errors, and some other minor changes, but no significant fabrications of the stupendous scale which would be required to concoct the story of Jesus' death.

Likewise when the Dead Sea Scrolls were discovered they included Hebrew Biblical scrolls dating from before the time of Jesus. These too agreed very closely with the oldest Hebrew Masoretic manuscripts of more than a thousand years later. Again, no fabrications, but everywhere you look, there is evidence of remarkably faithful copying.

Yeshua of Nazareth, a figure of history

Clearly there are events recorded in connection with Jesus' life that many non-Christians will not accept, such as the miracles, the virgin birth, and the resurrection. However what is beyond dispute is that Yeshua (Jesus) of Nazareth was a figure of history, who lived, attracted a following in his life time amongst his fellow Jews and was executed by crucifixion by the Roman authorities, after which his followers spread rapidly. Both secular and Christian sources of the period agree on this.

The primary sources for the history of Jesus' public life are the Gospels. These were written down relatively soon after his death – within living memory – and we have every indication that these sources were accepted as reliable in the early Christian community during a period when many first and second hand witnesses to Jesus' life were still available.

We conclude that any statements about Isa (Jesus) in the Quran, made six centuries after Jesus' death, must be judged against the historical evidence from these first-century sources, and not vice versa.

Plundering History

When Muhammad linked the name of *Allah* to the religious histories of Judaism and Christianity, this was a way to claim them for himself, and for Islam. In the light of later events, the notion that Islam was the original religion, and that all preceding prophets were Muslims, can be understood as an attempt to appropriate the histories of other religions to himself. This was a political move, and its purpose was to rob Christianity and Judaism of their own histories.

To this day many Biblical sites, such as the tombs of the Hebrew Patriarchs and the Temple Mount, are claimed by Islam as Muslim sites, not Jewish or Christian ones. After all, the Quran tells us that Abraham was 'a Muslim'. Under Islamic rule all Jews and Christians were banned from such sites. For example the tomb of Abraham was off limits to non-Muslims right up until modern times. The first non-Muslim to be admitted to this tomb since the Crusaders was the Prince of Wales, as late as the nineteenth century.

The place of the Jewish scriptures in Christianity is completely different from the place of the Bible in Islam

There is a fundamental difference between Christian attitudes to the Jewish scriptures and Islamic attitudes to the Bible. Christians accept the Hebrew scriptures. They were the scriptures of Jesus and the apostles. They were the scriptures of the early church. The whole of Christian belief and practice rests upon them. Core Christian concepts such as 'Messiah' (Greek *Christos*),

Although the Quran purports to 'verify' all earlier prophetic revelation, it is oblivious to the real contents of the Bible.

'Spirit of God', 'Kingdom of God', 'gospel' and 'salvation' are deeply rooted in the Hebrew Biblical traditions.

We note also that Christian seminaries devote considerable effort to studying the Hebrew scriptures. This is an integral part of training for Christian ministry. The Hebrew scriptures are read (in translation) every Sunday in churches all around the world.

In contrast the traditional mainstream Islamic treatment of the Bible is one of complete disregard. The Bible is not a part of the traditional curriculum of imams. Although the Quran purports to 'verify' all earlier prophetic revelation, it is oblivious to the real contents of the Bible. The claim that Christians and Jews deliberately corrupted their scriptures is made without evidence, and this only serves to cover up the Quran's historical inadequacies.

Some contemporary Muslim voices on Jesus

Muslim leaders and writers today continue to teach and preach the Islamic Jesus:

- Yasser Arafat, addressing a press conference at the United Nations in 1983, called Jesus 'the first Palestinian *fedayeen* who carried his sword' i.e. Jesus was a 'freedom fighter' or jihadist for Islam!

- Shaikh Ibrahim Madhi, employee of the Palestinian Authority, broadcast live in April 2002 on Palestinian Authority television:

  > 'The Jews await the false Jewish Messiah, while we await, with Allah's help...Jesus, peace be upon him. Jesus's pure hands will murder the false Jewish Messiah. Where? In the city of Lod, in Palestine.'[15]

  This passage is especially ironic in its symbolism. It has the 'true' Muslim messiah murdering the 'false' Jewish messiah, who is to be the anti-Christ figure. In fact it is the truly Jewish Jesus of Nazareth whose identity and message is supplanted by the Islamic Isa of the Quran, the destroyer of Christianity.

- Author Shamim A. Siddiqi of Flushing, New York put the classical position of Islam towards Christianity clearly in a letter to Daniel Pipes, *New York Post* columnist:

  > Abraham, Moses, Jesus, and Muhammad were all prophets of Islam. Islam is the common heritage of the Judeo-Christian-Muslim community of America, and establishing the Kingdom of God is the joint responsibility of

---

15   Memri Special Dispatch Series No. 370. Friday Sermon on Palestinian Authority TV.

all three Abrahamic faiths. Islam was the *din* (faith, way of life) of both Jews and Christians, who later lost it through human innovations. Now the Muslims want to remind their Jewish and Christian brothers and sisters of their original *din*. These are the facts of history.[16]

This historical negationism – appearing to affirm Christianity and Judaism whilst in fact rejecting and supplanting them – is a linchpin of Muslim apologetics. What is being affirmed is in fact neither Christianity nor Judaism, but Jesus as a prophet of Islam, Abraham as a Muslim, Moses as a Muslim etc. This is intended to lead to 'reversion' of Christians and Jews to Islam, which is what Siddiqi refers to when he speaks of 'the joint responsibility' of Jews and Christians to establish 'the Kingdom of God'. By this he is asserting that American Christians and Jews should embrace Islam and work together to establish sharia law and the dominance of Islam in the United States.

> The legend of Isa of the Quran is based on no recognized form of historical evidence.

A different gospel

Paul, in his letter to the Galatians, warns believers of the danger of abandoning the gospel of Jesus Christ:

> *I am astonished that you are so quickly deserting the one who called you by the grace of Christ and are turning to a different gospel – which is really no gospel at all. Evidently some people are throwing you into confusion and are trying to pervert the*

16   Siddiqi, Letter to the editor, *Commentary*, February 2002.

gospel of Christ. But even if we or an angel from heaven should preach a gospel other than the one we preached to you, let him be eternally condemned! (Galatians 1:6–8)

It is quite clear that the Injil, as described by the Quran, is nothing but a 'different gospel'. The prophet Isa (Jesus) of the Quran is a product of fable, imagination and ignorance. When Muslims venerate this Isa, they are far removed from Yeshua, the Jesus of the Bible and of history. The legend of Isa of the Quran is based on no recognized form of historical evidence, but on fables current in seventh century Arabia at the time of Muhammad, and on Muhammad's own desire to co-opt the Bible to support his new creed.

For most faithful Muslims Isa is the only Jesus they know. But if you accept this Muslim 'Jesus', and his 'gospel', then you also accept the Quran, and you accept Islam. Belief in this Isa is won at the cost of the libel that Jews and Christians have corrupted their scriptures, a charge that is without historical support. Belief in this Isa implies that much of Christian and Jewish history is in fact Islamic history.

The Jesus of history – the Jesus of the Gospels – is the foundation upon which Christianity developed. By Islamicising him, and making of him a Muslim prophet who preached the Quran, Islamic orthodoxy would destroy Christianity and take over its history. It does the same to Judaism.

In the end times as described by Muhammad, Isa the Muslim Jesus becomes a warrior who will return with his bloody sword and lance. He will destroy the Christian religion and make Islam the only religion in all the world. Finally, at the last judgement, he will condemn Christians to hell for believing in the crucifixion and the incarnation. These final acts of the Muslim Isa reflect Islam's traditional apologetic strategy in relation to Christianity, which is to deny the Yeshua of history, and replace him with a facsimile of Muhammad, so that nothing remains but Muhammad's Islam.

The Muslim supersessionist current claims that the whole biblical history of Israel and Christianity is Islamic history, that all the Prophets, Kings of Israel and Judea, and Jesus were Muslims. That the People of the Book should dare to challenge this statement is intolerable arrogance for an Islamic theologian. Jews and Christians are thus deprived of their Holy Scriptures and of their salvific value.[17]

17   Bat Ye'or, *Islam and Dhimmitude: where civilizations collide*, p.370.

PART TWO

The Holy Spirit, or Ruh Al-Qudus?

In this section the Ruh Al-Qudus or 'holy spirit' of the Quran is investigated and compared with the Holy Spirit of YHWH of the Bible.

Ruh Al-Qudus in the Quran

Do Muslims have the Holy Spirit?

The Answering Christianity web site offers a procedure for converting Christians to Islam. It comprises the following steps:

- 'I'd first prove to them that trinity is a man-made lie …

- 'Then, I'd prove to them that the Bible is corrupted and altered …

- 'Then, I'd show them what parts of the Bible do Muslims believe are closest to the Truth …

- 'Then, I'd prove to them that Muhammad and the Religion of Islam were foretold in the Bible.

- 'Then, I'd concentrate on the Oneness of GOD.

- 'I'd then show them the place and status of Jesus, Jews, Christians and non-Muslims in Islam.

- 'Last, if they start sharing their personal stories about how GOD Almighty saved them from danger or trouble, and how the Holy Spirit was there for them and inspired them, then I would tell them that Allah Almighty can still love them and have the Holy Spirit guide them and save them from trouble...'[18]

Who is this 'holy spirit' – in Arabic *Ruh Al-Qudus* – who is being offered to converts to Islam?

The Arabic word *ruh* means 'breath', 'spirit' or 'soul'. In the Quran there are repeated references to a *Ruh Al-Qudus* 'the Holy Spirit', or simply to *ruh* 'spirit'; however the way the Quran uses this expression 'holy spirit' is not consistent. It is possible to discern a number of different meanings for the word *ruh*, including an angel, a creative word from Allah, or the 'breath of life'.

The Quranic ruh 'spirit' as the angel Jibril (Gabriel)

One of the contexts in the Quran in which a 'spirit' is mentioned is the announcement to Maryam, mother of Isa, that she will bear a son. A 'spirit' is sent from Allah and appears in perfect human form to Maryam to announce the birth of Isa:

> And mention in the Book Maryam when she withdrew from her people to an eastern place, and she took a veil apart from them; then We sent unto her Our Spirit that presented himself to her a man without fault. She said 'I take refuge in the All-merciful from thee! ...' He said 'I am but a messenger come from thy Lord, to give thee a boy most pure.' (Q19:15–19)

18   'What is the best way to convert a Christian to Islam?' www.answering-christianity.com/convert_christians.htm

This messenger is certainly understood to be an angel, and the story is reminiscent of the account in Luke's Gospel of the angel Gabriel coming to Mary and bringing the announcement of Jesus' birth (Luke 1:26–38). Ibn Ishaq, Muhammad's biographer, tells a story that when a group of rabbis came to question Muhammad, they ask him: 'Tell us about the Spirit'. Muhammad replies, 'Do you not know that it is Gabriel, he who comes to me', and the rabbis reply, 'Agreed!'[19] This view, that the 'Spirit' is the angel Gabriel, is widely held among Muslims today.

Other Quranic references to a 'spirit' also make sense if the Ruh Al-Qudus is the angel Jibril. It was Jibril's role to bring the revelation of the Quran to Muhammad:

> ...Jibril – he it was that brought it down upon thy heart by the leave of Allah, confirming what was before it, and for a guidance and good tidings to the believers. (Q2:90–94)

And indeed we find a reference to the 'Holy Spirit' in exactly the same terms:

> [To Muhammad] Say: 'The Holy Spirit sent it [the Quran] down from thy Lord in truth, and to confirm those who believe, and to be a guidance and good tidings to those who surrender.' (Q16:100–104)

The 'Holy Spirit' is spoken of in the following passages is the same terms. These then can be understood to refer to the angel Jibril, bringing revelation:

> We gave to Musa the Book...and We gave Isa son of Maryam the clear signs, and confirmed him with the Holy Spirit... (Q2:80–84)

> When Allah said, Isa Son of Maryam, remember My blessing upon thee and upon thy mother, when I confirmed thee with the Holy Spirit, to speak to men in the cradle and of age...' (Q5:105–109)

---

19 Guillaume, *The Life of Muhammad*, p.255.

The following reference to the 'Faithful Spirit' must also be the angel Jibril:

> Truly it is the revelation of the Lord of all Being, brought down by the Faithful Spirit upon thy heart, that thou mayest be one of the warners, in a clear, Arabic tongue. (Q26:190–194)

There are also other 'spirit' references in the Quran which appear to refer to a being who is the foremost among the angels, that is to say, the angel Jibril:

> Upon the day when the Spirit and the angels stand in ranks they shall speak not, save him to whom the All-merciful has given leave, and who speaks aright. (Q78:35–39)

> The Night of Power is better than a thousand months; in it the angels and the Spirit descend, by the leave of their Lord, upon every command. (Q97:1–4)

Based on Sura 97, and the standard interpretation of the 'Holy Spirit' as Jibril, Muslims believe that the angel Jibril may visit Muslims who are fasting and praying during the fasting month on the 'Night of Power'.

The Quranic ruh 'breath' as a creative word from Allah

Another meaning of Arabic *ruh* is 'breath'. This is the more basic meaning of the word. Following this sense, a 'breath' from Allah can refer to his divine speech, his spoken word. In a key passage Isa is himself referred to as both a 'word' and a 'breath' from Allah, making the equation quite explicit:

> People of the Book, go not beyond the bounds in your religion, and say not as to Allah but the truth. The Messiah, Isa son of Maryam, was only the Messenger of Allah, and His Word that He committed to Maryam, and a spirit ['breath'] from

Him. So believe in Allah and His Messengers, and say not 'Three.' (Q4:165–169; see also Q3:40–44, where Jesus is referred to as a 'Word' from Allah)

It is not possible that *ruh* could be interpreted here to refer to an angel! The polemical point of this passage is a message to Christians: Isa was not divine, but only a creature. Thus references to 'word' and 'breath' relate to the manner of Isa's creation. The Quran is saying that Allah created him by his very word. This, after all, is the standard position of the Quran on the way in which Allah creates things:

He is the All-creator, the All-knowing. His command, when He desires a thing, is to say to it 'Be,' and it is. (Q36:80–84)

So when Isa is spoken of as a word and a breath from Allah, this is a metaphor which emphasizes the mere humanity of a prophet, created by Allah's word.

The Quranic ruh the 'breath' of life

How then are we to understand the following passages, in which Allah is said to breathe into Maryam (Q21:90–94) or alternatively directly into her vulva (Q66:10–14)!

And she who guarded her virginity [furuj, lit. 'opening' or 'vulva'], so We breathed into her of our spirit and appointed her and her son to be a sign unto all beings. (Q21:90–94)

And Maryam, Imran's daughter, who guarded her virginity [furuj], so We breathed into it of our spirit, and she confirmed the Words of her Lord and His Books, and became one of the obedient. (Q66:10–14)

These verses of the Quran are reminiscent of Matthew 1:20, in which an angel tells Joseph to marry Mary because 'what is conceived in her is from the Holy Spirit'. However what is different is the physicality of the breath of Allah, which goes into Maryam, causing her conception. Note the grammatical difference between the two passages, with one referring to the breath going into *her*, whilst in the other the breath enters *it*, i.e. her vulva.

We can be certain that the whole point of these passages is that Isa – a messenger, Maryam's son, and not divine – was a mere creation, formed within Maryam's womb. Thus 'breath' here could well be interpreted as referring to a creative word of Allah, in the manner just seen for Jesus the 'word' and 'breath' of Allah.

However there is another more likely interpretation for these passages, that the 'breath' of Allah is a reference to the breath of life, apparently borrowing the language of the creation narrative in Genesis:

> *...YHWH God formed the man from the dust of the ground and breathed into his nostrils the breath of life, and the man became a living being.* (Genesis 2:7)

This understanding of 'breath' is suggested by the Quranic passages:

> *See, I am creating a mortal of a clay of mud moulded. When I have shaped him, and breathed My spirit in him, fall you down, bowing before him!* (Q15:25–29)

> *He originated the creation of man out of clay, then He fashioned his progeny of an extraction of mean water, then He shaped him, and breathed His spirit in him.* (Q32:5–9)

Such a use of *ruh* is quite exceptional for the Quran, which normally does not allow human beings to have any participation with Allah, as we shall see. That Allah's breath could go 'into' someone reflects the Biblical understanding of a God who can indwell people, not the dominant understanding of Allah in the Quran.

Only 'a little' known about the Spirit?

At one point Muhammad is apparently warned that people will ask him about the Spirit. The answer, he is told, is that the Spirit is a mystery about which he has been given little knowledge:

> *They will question thee concerning the Spirit. Say: 'The Spirit is of the bidding of my Lord. You have been given of knowledge nothing except a little.'* (Q17:85–89)

It is an irony that Muhammad should say this, because in the Bible there is a wealth of information about the Holy Spirit of God. This subject is not one about which God has given humanity little knowledge.

The Holy Spirit in the Bible

In the Bible the 'Spirit of God', 'Spirit of the Lord', or 'Holy Spirit' certainly does not refer to an angel, but to the powerful, life-giving and creative presence of the living God.

According to the Letter to the Hebrews, angels are 'ministering spirits' who serve both God and 'those who will inherit salvation'.

Consider that when Gabriel announces to Mary that she is going to conceive, this will take place, the angel says, when the 'Holy Spirit will come upon you, and the power of the Most High will overshadow

> Muhammad took many elements of his religious beliefs and practices over from the Jews and Christians he met in Mecca and Medina.

you' (Luke 1:35). Clearly here the angel Gabriel and the Spirit are quite distinct, and indeed the angel Gabriel is subordinate to the Holy Spirit, serving as his messenger.

The Holy Spirit here is not a reference to God's word, but to the presence of God, which will 'overshadow' and 'come upon' Mary.

Muhammad apparently derived his mistaken conception of the 'Holy Spirit' from the accounts of Christians, confusing references to the Holy Spirit with angels or other spirits. Muhammad took many elements of his religious beliefs and practices over from the Jews and Christians he met in Mecca and Medina. In this particular case, as in others, he does not understand what he hears, and the Quran reflects his confusion.

This confusion reflects a deep issue concerning the understanding of Allah in Islam. Islamic theology cannot conceive of Allah being present or 'indwelling' any person or place. Allah of the Quran cannot personally visit anyone. his is why the coming of the Holy Spirit to Mary gets misinterpreted as an angel. This matter will be taken up more fully in the next chapter. However for now we will consider why Christians say that the Holy Spirit of the Bible is God.

The identity of the Holy Spirit was a topic of ancient discussion by Christian theologians. The early church fathers Basil and Athanasius gave arguments that the Spirit of God is divine.

Athanasius on why the Holy Spirit is God

In the fourth century AD, Athanasius responded to the arguments of a group he referred to as the *Tropikoi* because they preferred figurative interpretations – tropes - for some Biblical references to the Holy Spirit. They had formerly been Arians, denying the deity of Christ. Later, when then came to agree that Christ was one with God, they still had problems with the deity of the Holy Spirit.

Athanasius addressed their concerns in letters he wrote to Serapion.[20]

One of the Tropikoi's claims was that the Spirit is an angel, a created being. In response Athanasius pointed out what we have already seen, that in the annunciation to Mary, it is the angel Gabriel who serves the Holy Spirit.

Other reasons Athanasius gives that the Holy Spirit is not an angel or some kind of created being are as follows:

- The Spirit is never spoken of in the Bible as an angel, despite plenty of opportunities (in fact hundreds).

- The role of angels is to serve God, and in Zechariah an angel serves the Holy Spirit by testifying to his work:

    > He [the angel] answered, "Do you not know what these are?" "No, my lord," I replied. So he said to me, "This is the word of YHWH to Zerubbabel: 'Not by might, nor by power, but by my Spirit,' says YHWH Almighty." (Zechariah 4:5–6)

- Isaiah identified the Holy Spirit with the presence of God in Israel, leading and guiding the people to the promised land:

    > Then his people recalled the days of old, of Moses and his people – where is he who brought them through the sea, with the shepherd of his flock? Where is he who set his Holy Spirit among them, who sent his glorious arm of power to be at Moses' right hand, who divided the waters before them, to gain for himself everlasting renown, who led them through the depths? Like a horse in open country,

---

20   Shapland, *The letters of Saint Athanasius concerning the Holy Spirit*.

they did not stumble; like cattle that go down to the plain, they were given rest by the Spirit of YHWH. That is how you guided your people to make for yourself a glorious name. (Isaiah 63:11–14)

- The testimony of Exodus confirms that the presence of the Spirit guiding the Israelites could not have been a angel. In fact, after the incident with the golden calf, God had offered to send an angel to accompany the people of Israel, saying it would be too dangerous for God himself to be among them:

> *Then YHWH said to Moses, 'Leave this place, you and the people you brought up out of Egypt, and go to the land I promised on oath to Abraham, Isaac, and Jacob, saying, "I will give it to your descendants." I will send an angel before you and drive out the Canaanites, Amorites, Hittites, Perizzites, Hivites, and Jebusites. Go up to a land flowing with milk and honey. But I will not go with you, because you are a stiff-necked people and I might destroy you on the way.' When the people heard these distressing words, they began to mourn and no one put on any ornaments.* (Exodus 33:1–4)

Moses and the people were not happy with this offer. As Athanasius writes 'Moses too knew that angels are creatures'. Instead Moses said he only wished to proceed if the very presence of the Lord would go with them. God agrees to this:

> *Moses said to YHWH, 'You have been telling me, "Lead this people," but you have not let me know whom you will send with me. You have said, "I know*

you by name, and you have found favour with me." If you are pleased with me, teach me your ways, so I may know you and continue to find favour with you. Remember that this nation is your people.' YHWH replied, 'My Presence will go with you, and I will give you rest.' Then Moses said to him, 'If your Presence does not go with us, do not send us up from here. How will anyone know that you are pleased with me and with your people, unless you go with us? What else will distinguish me and your people from all the other people on the face of the earth?' And YHWH said to Moses, 'I will do the very thing you have asked, because I am pleased with you, and I know you by name.' (Exodus 33:12–17)

Athanasius writes of these discussions between God and Moses: 'when the Spirit was with the people, God was with them'.

- Continuing this theme, Paul speaks of the 'temple of God' as the temple of the Spirit: where the Spirit is, God himself is present:

    Do you not know that you yourselves are God's temple and that God's Spirit lives in you? If anyone destroys God's temple, God will destroy him; for God's temple is sacred, and you are that temple. (1 Corinthians 3:16)

- Creatures are sanctified – made holy – and renewed by the Spirit (Psalm 10:30, Romans 1:4, 1 Corinthians 6:11, Titus 3:4–7, Hebrews 6:4), but the Spirit is not himself spoken of as one who is made holy or renewed. So the Spirit cannot be one of the creatures.

- The Spirit gives life (Romans 8:11, Acts 3:15, John 4:14, 7:39). Who gives life, but is not himself given life, cannot be a creature.

- The scriptures teach us that by partaking in the Spirit we share in the Son and the Father (1 John 4:13, 2 Peter 1:4). If the Holy Spirit were a creature we would have no participation in God through sharing in the Spirit.

- Through the Spirit all things are created (Psalm 104:29–30). 'All things' cannot be created through a creature.

- The Spirit is eternal:

  > ...how much more, then, will the blood of Christ, who through the eternal Spirit offered himself unblemished to God, cleanse our consciences from acts that lead to death, so that we may serve the living God! (Hebrews 9:14)

- The Spirit fills all things. It is not in the nature of a creature to be omnipresent:

  > Where can I go from your Spirit? Where can I flee from your presence? (Psalm 139:7)

Basil on why the Holy Spirit is God

The scriptures teach us that by partaking in the Spirit we share in the Son and the Father.

Basil also wrote in the fourth century, but a generation after Athanasius. Earlier in his ministry Basil had been reticent to speak about the distinctiveness of the Spirit, however later in his life he wrote *On the Holy*

Spirit, a famous statement of classical Christian belief.[21] In it Basil argued that the Spirit was to be worshipped and glorified, along with the Father and the Son.

One of Basil's arguments was based upon the great commission of Matthew, in which the disciples of Christ are called to baptise people in the name of the Father, the Son and the Holy Spirit (Matthew 28:19). The very covenant of Christian baptism is founded upon the unity of the Father and the Son with the Holy Spirit, Basil argued.

Other arguments presented by Basil for the deity of the Spirit and his unity with the Father and the Son included:

- The Bible speaks of the presence of the Spirit of prophecy as the presence of God:

> *But if an unbeliever or someone who does not understand comes in while everybody is prophesying, he will be convinced by all that he is a sinner and will be judged by all, and the secrets of his heart will be laid bare. So he will fall down and worship God, exclaiming, "God is really among you!"* (1 Corinthians 14:24–25)

- Lying to God is lying to the Spirit:

> [The story of Ananias and Sapphira:] *"Didn't it belong to you before it was sold? And after it was sold, wasn't the money at your disposal? What made you think of doing such a thing? You have not lied to men but to God."… Peter said to her, "How could you agree to test the Spirit of the Lord? Look! The feet of the men who buried your husband are at the door, and they will carry you out also."* (Acts 5:4, 9)

---

21   Basil, *On the Holy Spirit*, in *Nicene and Post-Nicene Fathers*, second series.

- The Spirit's relation to God is to be understood as a person's relation to his own spirit. This means that the Spirit cannot be a creature or outside of and separate from God:

  > For who among men knows the thoughts of a man except the man's spirit within him? In the same way no one knows the thoughts of God except the Spirit of God. (1 Corinthians 2:11)

- In his first letter to the Corinthians, Paul describes the unified working of the gifts of God which is based upon the unity of God: they are activated in every believer by 'the same God' or, alternatively, by 'one and the same Spirit':

  > There are different kinds of gifts, but the same Spirit. There are different kinds of service, but the same Lord. There are different kinds of working, but the same God works all of them in all men. (1 Corinthians 12:4–6)

  > All these are the work of one and the same Spirit, and he gives them to each one, just as he determines. (1 Corinthians 12:11)

- The Spirit is called 'Lord', the title for God himself:

  > But their minds were made dull, for to this day the same veil remains when the old covenant is read. It has not been removed, because only in Christ is it taken away. Even to this day when Moses is read, a veil covers their hearts. But whenever anyone turns to the Lord, the veil is taken away. Now the Lord is the

Spirit, and where the Spirit of the Lord is, there is freedom. (2 Corinthians 3:14–17)

- The scriptures are described as 'God-inspired' and 'Spirit-inspired' at one and the same time:

   All Scripture is God-breathed and is useful for teaching, rebuking, correcting and training in righteousness... (2 Timothy 3:16)

   For prophecy never had its origin in the will of man, but men spoke from God as they were carried along by the Holy Spirit. (2 Peter 1:21)

Conclusion: the Quranic Ruh Al-Qudus is not God; the Biblical Holy Spirit is God

We have found that the Islamic notion of the 'holy spirit' (what little we are allowed to know) as a created being is deeply at odds with the Bible's fulsome teaching about the Spirit as the personal and powerful presence of YHWH.

It is good to be reminded of Jesus' words that all sins may be forgiven, but to sin against the Holy Spirit, to blaspheme against His holiness and majesty, is a sin which cannot be forgiven:

> Throughout the Bible, the Holy Spirit is revealed as the creating, life-giving, renewing, sanctifying presence of the living God.

I tell you the truth, all the sins and blasphemies of men will be forgiven them. But whoever blasphemes against the Holy Spirit will never be forgiven; he is guilty of an eternal sin. (Mark 3:28–9).

It would be nonsensical for Christ to say such a thing about an angel. Jesus made this statement when some were accusing him of driving out demons by the hand of Satan. This ministry of deliverance, he had explained elsewhere, was done by the power of the Spirit, and Jesus is saying that to deny the Spirit of God glory and honour is a terrible and serious thing.

Throughout the Bible, the Holy Spirit is revealed as the creating, life-giving, renewing, sanctifying presence of the living God. It is nonsense to separate the Spirit off from God as one of his creatures. Worse than this, it is blasphemy. The Spirit is no angel, nor any other kind of creature, but the power and presence of God himself. The Christian doctrine, that the Holy Spirit is God himself, and together with the Son and the Father, worthy of all praise and glory, is a faithful response to the consistent testimony of the scriptures.

PART THREE

Who is the LORD God?

In this section we consider whether the identity of God is the same as that of Allah of the Quran. We will examine whether the character or personality of YHWH is the same as that of Allah as portrayed in the Quran.

What Is At Stake?

We can now consider the question of whether Allah of the Quran is the God of the Bible. What should Christians make of the claim that 'We all worship the same God'? More and more people are asking whether the God of the Quran (Allah) and the God of the Bible (YHWH) are the same. What is the truth?

A cornerstone of Islamic doctrine

It is a core doctrine of Islam that Allah is the God of the Bible: to be a true Muslim one must believe that they are the same. The Quran insists on this, the hadiths insist on it, and all Muslim scholars agree on it. In Islam this is not a conclusion derived by study or something proved by argument: it known by revelation from Allah himself.

Can this view be tested? Since the Quran denies the genuineness and authority of the Bible as it exists today, from the conservative Islamic perspective there can be no grounds to question this core belief. Without having access to the original text of the Bible, there can be no basis for comparing the Bible with the Quran, or the God of the Bible with Allah. The traditional Islamic view is that if you want to know what the God of the Bible is like, then read the Quran.

Not only must Muslims believe that 'we worship the same God', but this message is always a central component of the presentation of Islam to Christians and Jews. Islamic mission or *dawa* presents this message loud and clear, and it is partly because of this that Christians are being forced to consider this question in our present day.

The message that we do worship one and the same God provides the linchpin of Muslims' efforts to convert the 'people of the Book' to the faith of Muhammad. In addition, this belief, once accepted, can lead Christians to support Islamic perspectives in ways other than conversion. For example, embracing this Islamic doctrine wins a measure of respect and even support for Islam from Christians. The holding of many 'Abrahamic Faith' conferences throughout the world is but one expression of the Islamicisation of Christian thought about interfaith dialogue.

But should Christians accept this Islamic dogma? And if not, why not? How should Christians respond to this claim, this fundamental point of Muslim doctrine? Should we import this Islamic doctrine into our belief system, and reshape our religious world view accordingly?

This is a very important matter. Not only does it relate to the question of whether Christians and Jews should convert to Islam, but it raises deeper issues concerning the very character of YHWH and Allah. No-one can truly understand the nature of a faith without engaging with the very essence of the identity of their god. Christians will never understand Islam until they understand who Allah is, and Muslims will never understand Christianity until they engage with the character of YHWH as revealed in the Bible.

How then can we make this comparison? We cannot compare the bodies or photographs of Allah and YHWH; no fingerprint tests are possible; nor DNA comparisons. But we can ask such questions as:

- Do these two have the same personality?

- Have they acted and spoken consistently?

- Do they have the same potential for relationship with human beings?

Before we explore such questions we will consider where the names YHWH and Allah come from, and what they mean. We also must make reference to an idea which Christians have been tempted by down the ages: Marcionism.

Marcionism not an option

Marcion (b.AD110) came to believe that the Bible described two different gods. There was the god of the Old Testament, and the god of the New Testament. The details of Marcion's belief-system do not concern us. However what is

> Not only must Muslims believe that 'we worship the same God', but this message is always a central component of the presentation of Islam to Christians and Jews.

of relevance is that many people today in post-Christian societies have moved to a marcionite position, typically on the basis of a poor understanding of the scriptures. Some say that the god of the Old Testament is judgmental and vindictive, whilst the god of the New Testament is loving and forgiving. Some even suggest that the god of Islam is the 'Old Testament god'. They completely forget that the God of Jesus was YHWH of the Hebrew scriptures.

Such teachings are clearly sub-Christian – indeed they completely undermine Christian doctrine – yet they have a powerful resonance in western culture today.

We do not need to offer a full response to Marcionism here. However it is helpful to point out in advance that, as we consider the attributes of YHWH which distinguish him so clearly from Allah of the Quran, these very attributes will be shown to be deeply grounded in the Old Testament, and consistently demonstrated in the New Testament as well.

The Divine Name

The name Allah

Although many Arabic Christians today refer to YHWH as Allah, there is no evidence that the Arabic name *Allah* (or any dialect variant of it) was used by Arab Christians or Jews in Arabia as the personal name of God before the time of Muhammad.[22]

Allah is announced as God's name in the Quran, and is referred to 2,700 times:

> *"Who is the Lord of the Heavens and of the earth?"*
> *Say "Allah." (Q13:15–19)*

The word *Allah* is derived linguistically by a contraction of the Arabic expression *al-ilah* 'the god', which would have been a generic expression used for gods in general. The word *ilah* comes from an ancient Semitic root reflected also in the Hebrew *Elohim* ('God, gods').

It seems that *Allah* had previously been used as the title of a pagan Arabian deity known to the Meccans before the time of Muhammad. Reasons for believing this are that:

---

22   What there is evidence to support is that related languages used cognate forms, e.g. Aramaic *Alaha* to refer to the God of the Bible.

- The feminine form of Allah, derived in parallel fashion from *al-ilat* 'the goddess' was the title of a specific idol known among the Arabs:

  > They then adopted Allat as their goddess. Allat stood in al-Ta'if, and was more recent than Manah. She was a cubic rock beside which a certain Jew used to prepare his barley porridge (sawiq). Her custody was in the hands of the banu-'Attab ibn-Malik of the Thaqif, who had built an edifice over her. The Quraysh, as well as all the Arabs, were wont to venerate Allat. They also used to name their children after her, calling them Zayd-Allat and Taym-Allat.[23]

- Muhammad's pagan father, who died before Muhammad was born, bore the name *Abd Allah* (*Abdullah*), 'slave of Allah'. This suggests that Allah was the principal deity of Muhammad's grandfather, since it was a common practice among the pagans to name their children after their personal god.

- Pagan assumptions about Allah were very much a live issue during Muhammad's prophetic career, because the Quran repeatedly seeks to counter claims that Allah was but one among many gods; that he had divine sons or daughters; or that the jinn – demonic beings – shared divinity with him. Q53:19–24 refutes the pagan idea that the goddesses al-Uzza, al-Ilat and Manat were the 'daughters of Allah'.[24] Furthermore Q37:145–59 rejects any suggestion that Allah has sons and daughters, that angels could be female, being capable of reproducing, or that the jinn (demons)

---

23   Faris, *The book of idols*, p.14.

24   Al-Tabari, *Jami' al-Bay'dn fi Tafsir al-Qur'an*, vol.27, pp.34–36. Also Winnett, 'The Daughters of Allah'.

share kinship with Allah (see also Q16:59, Q6:100).

- It does seem from certain verses of the Quran that the pagan Arabs regarded the god Allah as the creator of the world, god of the heavens, the weather and the waters, but that they had other gods in their pantheon beside this god of the wind and the waves:

> If thou askest them, 'Who created the heavens and the earth and subjected the sun and the moon?' they will say, 'Allah.' How then are they perverted?
>
> If thou askest them, 'Who sends down out of heaven water, and therewith revives the earth after it is dead?' they will say 'Allah.'
>
> When they embark in the ships, they call on Allah, making their religion sincerely His; but when He has delivered them to the land, they associate others with Him, that they may be ungrateful for what We have given them, and take their enjoyment; they will soon know!' (Q29:60–69; see also Q39:35–39)

What else can we know about the pagan deity associated with the name of Allah? Some have identified Allah with the moon god, although the evidence for this seems tenuous.[25]

There is some possibility that *Hubal*, the 'Lord' of the Quraysh (Muhammad's tribe) and the chief deity in the Kaaba (the pagan sanctuary at Mecca), could have been

---

25   The often-repeated claim that the crescent moon derives from moon-god worship appears to be a mistake. This symbol was taken over from the Byzantines after Constantinople was conquered by the Turks.

a manifestation of Allah.[26] This could help account for the continued use of the Kaaba in Islam for the worship of Allah, for Hubal's idol was located in the centre of the sanctuary beside the Zamzam sacred well.

We also know from Ibn Ishaq's biography of Muhammad that his family were devotees of Hubal. Muhammad's grandfather, Abdul Mutallib, had undertaken to sacrifice Muhammad's father to Hubal[27] – this was the same youth Abd Allah whose name showed that he had been dedicated to the god Allah. Muhammad himself was dedicated as an infant before the statue of Hubal by the same grandfather.[28] There is even an account of Muhammad's grandfather praying to Allah beside the idol of Hubal while lots are being cast to determine which son he will sacrifice.[29]

> YHWH was revealed to Moses as God's name at the burning bush. This name, God tells Moses, is 'my name forever'.

Although the name Allah was adapted from Arab paganism, Muhammad categorically rejected any association between Allah and the old idols, as he sought to cleanse the worship of Allah from what he regarded as its pagan accretions. The idol of Hubal was destroyed, along with all the other idols, when Muhammad conquered Mecca and took control of the Kaaba. Although it is interesting to speculate about the origins of *Allah* in the pagan period before Muhammad, it is ultimately secondary to the question of the identity of Allah, which must be based upon an examination of the Quran.

---

26   Guillaume, *The Life of Muhammad*, p.64
27   Guillaume, *The Life of Muhammad*, pp.67–68.
28   Guillaume, *The Life of Muhammad*, p.70.
29   Guillaume, *The Life of Muhammad*, p.67.

The name YHWH

The proper name of God in the Bible, *YHWH*, is written with consonants only, and in Jewish tradition is never pronounced. The Jewish manner of reading from the Bible is to substitute the word *Adonai* ('lord') for YHWH. *Yahweh* and *Jehovah* are Christian expansions of YHWH with vowels added.[30] Here I will refer to the LORD God of the Bible as YHWH or simply 'the LORD', following a standard English Bible translation convention.

YHWH was revealed to Moses as God's name at the burning bush. This name, God tells Moses, is 'my name forever'.

> *Moses said to God, 'Suppose I go to the Israelites and say to them, "The God of your fathers has sent me to you" and they ask me, "What is his name" Then what shall I tell them?'* God said to Moses, 'I am who I am. [or 'I will be who I will be.'] *This is what you are to say to the Israelites: "I AM has sent me to you."'* God also said to Moses, 'Say to the Israelites "YHWH, the God of your fathers – the God of Abraham, the God of Isaac and the God of Jacob – has sent me to you." This is my name forever, the name by which I am to be remembered from generation to generation.'* (Exodus 3:13–15)

The name is revealed again to Moses on Mount Sinai when he asks God to show his glory. The LORD replies 'you cannot see my face' (Exodus 33:20), and instead announces his name to Moses:

> *Then YHWH came down in the cloud and stood there with him and proclaimed his name 'YHWH'. And he passed in front of Moses, proclaiming, 'YHWH, YHWH, the compassionate and gracious*

---

30   Indeed *Jehovah* was a mistake, combining the consonants of *YHWH* with the vowels of *Adonai*.

God, slow to anger, abounding in love and faithfulness, maintaining love to thousands, and forgiving wickedness, rebellion and sin. Yet he does not leave the guilty unpunished; he punishes the children for the sin of the fathers to the third and fourth generation. (Exodus 34:5–7)

A Question of
Mistaken Identity

In a sense YHWH and Allah certainly claim to live at the same address: 'the creator of the universe'. Their names are not the same – YHWH and Allah – and here there is already a problem, because YHWH was supposed to have been God's name forever. But what about their identity?

We can see from the Bible and the Quran that YHWH and Allah share certain similarities. For example, they are both said to be to be the creator, all-powerful, merciful, and the judge of humanity. They both are said to speak to humanity, and to provide laws for people to live by. To take just one attribute, the Quran and the Bible – both the Old and New Testaments – again and again describe YHWH and Allah as a judge who will hold all people to account.

Whilst we could study the similarities between YHWH and Allah, and this would be an interesting study in itself, it is the differences which determine whether two individuals are the same. Any two human beings will share considerable similarities: two arms, two legs, one head, two kidneys, one heart and so forth. However to work out whether two individuals are the same we have to go beyond shared features and focus on look for their differences.

The authors Newton and Rafiqul Haqq make this very point in connection with the problem of discerning a counterfeit:

> When comparing two bank notes for the purpose of determining which is the counterfeit and which is the genuine – we must not concentrate on the similarities. For we will find that the two notes will almost look the same. But we must concentrate on the differences. For it is the differences which will prove which is the genuine one.[31]

Many ways to approach this question

As we have seen, Islamic dogma insists, as an article of faith, that Allah is the same deity as the God of the Bible. For a Christian, who does not accept Muhammad's claim that the Bible has been intentionally corrupted, such a claim can only be tested by comparing the teachings of the Bible with those of the Quran and the hadiths. There is a variety of ways to make this comparison. As various authors have shown, one can uncover many inconsistencies between the message of the Bible and the Quran. Four of these are surveyed here:

- Different principles for punishment
- Is God finished with the Jews?
- Different Bible stories
- Muhammad and Jesus – can their messages be reconciled?

31   *Allah: is he God?*, p.54.

Different principles for punishment

In their booklet *Allah: is he God?*, Newton and Rafiqul Haqq consider very carefully what Allah and YHWH have said about the punishment of thieves and the treatment of women, and they conclude on these grounds that the two gods must be different. The Bible's approach to punishing theft is to require restoration to the victim. The Quran's punishment for theft is amputation of the hand, and under conditions which show great moral inconsistency. They ask the question: 'How could the same god apply completely different principles for punishment in the Bible and the Quran?'

In fact Newton and Rafiqul Haqq go beyond this simple comparison, and lay bare the ethical values which underpin these very distinct penalties, arguing that they reflect deep discrepancies in the characters of Allah and YHWH.

Is God finished with the Jews?

One could raise other discrepancies between the judgements of YHWH and Allah. For example the Bible says that God's promises to Israel are irrevocable (Romans 11:29) and that he will never forget Israel or permanently turn his favour away from his people:

> *Can a mother forget the baby at her breast and have no compassion on the child she has borne? Though she may forget, I will not forget you! See, I have engraved you on the palms of my hands...* (Isaiah 49:15–16)

In the earlier verses of the Quran we do find a positive stance taken towards the Jews. However, over time, the words of Allah concerning the Jews turned sour, and the Quran's final message is that God has, with finality, rejected the Jews as a nation. Charges made against the Jews include that:

- The Jews have the worst hostility to Muslims. (Q5:85)

- They start wars and cause mayhem in the earth. (Q5:65–69)

- They rush around the earth doing evil. (Q5:65–69)

- They are cursed because they said Allah's hands are tied. (Q5:65–69)

- They are greedy for this life, and love it more than eternal life. (Q2:89–90)

- Allah cursed the Jews, turning them into monkeys and pigs for their evil deeds. (Q7:165–169, Q5:65–69, Q2:60–64)

- The prophets Dawud (David) and Isa (Jesus) have cursed the Jews. (Q5:80–84)

- Allah has cursed Jews for their unbelief. (Q4:49)

It is not credible that the same god would take such two contradictory positions towards the Jews. We will return to this matter when we consider the character of YHWH.

Different Bible stories

We have already seen that there are discrepancies between the Bible and the Quran. Mark Gabriel, a convert from Islam and a scholar in Islamic history, gives a list in his book *Islam and the Jews* of all the passages in the Quran which retell Bible stories. These comprise around 7% of the total text of the Quran. He reports many differences between what the Quran and the Bible say. If it was the same God inspiring Muhammad, and Muhammad was truly a prophet of Allah, then these discrepancies must mean the Bible is corrupt.

Gabriel's conclusion is however very different:

Here's what I believe: The original source for the prophet Muhammad's stories about Abraham and the other prophets is the Bible. I do not think the Quran is a new revelation from the same God who inspired the Bible. One reason is that the Quran and the Bible are often contradictory. I do not think God would choose to give new information that would contradict the record that He had established thousands of years earlier. The god Muhammad proclaimed does not exist.[32]

Muhammad and Jesus – can their messages be reconciled?

One can also point to many discrepancies between the life and teaching of Muhammad and Jesus. Quite apart from the profound

> "The god Muhammad proclaimed does not exist." - Mark Gabriel.

differences in the moral example of the two men, we find in several respects that aspects of the law which Jesus had set aside were to be reinstated by Muhammad:

- Jesus spoke against stoning adulterers, but Muhammad insisted that adulterers must be stoned. How could the one God first command stoning in the Torah, then abrogate it through the example of Christ, and then reinstate in through Muhammad?

- How could the one God first declare certain foods unclean in the Torah, then declare all foods clean through Christ, and then reinstate food taboos with Muhammad?

---

32   Mark Gabriel, *Islam and the Jews*, pp.84–85.

- How could Christ forbid the use of the sword and warn against the older world-view of hating enemies, whilst Muhammad, through the message of the Quran, gloried in the sword, and urged his followers to hate all those who rejected his message?

If the God of the Bible were indeed also speaking through Muhammad, such about-faces would imply the existence of deep inconsistencies within God's character. Such discrepancies therefore are evidence that Muhammad and Jesus Christ did not receive revelation from the same source.

We need to go deeper

It is not enough to just list symptoms of differences between YHWH and Allah. We must go deeper and gain a picture of the fundamental attributes of the creator, as reported in the Bible and the Quran. We will see that the very nature of these two beings are different. These differences are profound and concern the way God relates to his creation. It is essential to understand these if we are to appreciate the depth of the gulf separating the Bible's conception of YHWH and the Quran's conception of Allah.

In the following chapters we explore these questions:

- Is God the author of evil?
- Can God indwell people or places?
- Is God holy?
- Are people created in God's image or like God in any respects?
- Does God love, and who does he love?
- Is God faithful to his word?

The Author of Evil

This chapter is based upon Daniel Shayesteh's profound comparison of world religions in his book *A journey from 'gods' to Christ*. Shayesteh was an Iranian Revolutionary Guard, still a young man during Khomeini's revolution. As a political leader he fell foul of Khomeini, and found himself in an Iranian jail, suffering torture and contemplating his imminent death. Although he had been able to recite the Quran in Arabic from an early age, in Khomeini's prison Daniel began to read the Quran in his own language. What he read there caused him to lose his faith in Allah. One of his disturbing discoveries was that Allah presents himself as the author of evil, and he began to comprehend why his tormenters claimed to be torturing him in accordance with the teachings of the Quran.

Muslims must, as a matter of doctrine, believe in the uniqueness, and purity of Allah. However the statements in the Quran concerning the origin of sin in humanity, and even in Satan prove the opposite. Allah is the one who inspires debauchery in humanity:

> *By the soul and That which shaped it and inspired it to lewdness* [or 'debauchery'] *and godfearing!* (Q91:5–9)

Remarkably the very next verse after this declares that anyone who purifies his soul will prosper. Shayesteh has this to say:

> These are the major doctrinal problems in the Qur'an. Firstly, man will not be able to purify the mighty sin that has been inspired by Allah. Secondly, the call of Allah is not just, since he has filled man's heart with sin and caused him to commit sin.[33]

Not only this, but as Shayesteh points out, Allah has corrupted Satan to lead men and women into hell. The Quran says that Iblis (Satan) refused to bow down and worship Adam at Allah's command. As a result Allah humbled Satan and enacts retribution against him by subjecting him to be an agent for evil against humanity. Allah, the Quran says, 'perverts' Satan for the task of leading humanity into hell.

> *Said he [Satan to Allah], 'Now, for Thy perverting me, I shall surely sit in ambush for them on Thy straight path; then I shall come on them from before them and from behind them, from their right hands and their left hands; Thou wilt not find most of them thankful.'*
> *Said He [Allah], 'Go thou forth from it, despised and banished. Those of them that follow thee – I shall assuredly fill Hell with all of you.'* (Q7:10–14)

YHWH's eyes cannot look on evil

In contrast to Allah, YHWH has no partnership with evil, and cannot even look upon it:

> *He is the Rock, his works are perfect, and all his ways are just. A faithful God who does no wrong, upright and just is he.* (Deuteronomy 32:4)

> *You are not a God who takes pleasure in evil; with you the wicked cannot dwell.* (Psalm 5:4)

33   Shayesteh, *A journey from gods to Christ*, p.68.

The LORD is upright; he is my Rock, and there is no wickedness in him. (Psalm 92:15)

Your eyes are too pure to look on evil; you cannot tolerate wrong. (Habakkuk 1:13)

This is the message we have heard from him and declare to you: God is light; in him there is no darkness at all. (1 John 1:5)

In the Bible, evil is not something which God inspires in people. The essence of evil is rebellion against God and defiance of his will. God however is pure, good and true.

It must also be acknowledged that the question of whether God is the author of evil has taxed Christian theologians. It is reported in the Bible that YHWH can act to harden the hearts of the unrepentant. In the Exodus story, God hardens Pharaoh's heart so he would not relent during the plagues that befell Egypt (Exodus 7:3–22). Such a situation is referred to by Paul in his second letter to the Thessalonians where God's judgement is shown against the disobedient by maintaining them in a state of delusion:

> In contrast to Allah, YHWH has no partnership with evil, and cannot even look upon it.

For this reason God sends them a powerful delusion so that they will believe the lie and so that all will be condemned who have not believed the truth but have delighted in wickedness. (2 Thessalonians 2:11–12)

There is a remarkable passage when God even commissions a 'lying spirit' to mislead King Ahab. Nevertheless, despite doing this, God has the Prophet

Micaiah reveal to Ahab what has been happening, a warning which Ahab chooses to ignore:

> Micaiah continued, "Therefore hear the word of the LORD: I saw the LORD sitting on his throne with all the host of heaven standing around him on his right and on his left. And the LORD said, 'Who will entice Ahab into attacking Ramoth Gilead and going to his death there?' One suggested this, and another that. Finally, a spirit came forward, stood before the LORD and said, 'I will entice him.' 'By what means?' the LORD asked. 'I will go out and be a lying spirit in the mouths of all his prophets,' he said. 'You will succeed in enticing him,' said the LORD. 'Go and do it.' So now the LORD has put a lying spirit in the mouths of all these prophets of yours. The LORD has decreed disaster for you." (1 Kings 22:19–23)

These passages show that God's judgement is an evil thing for whose who fall under it, and when people walk outside of his protection through disobedience, they lay themselves open, under God's will, to the power of evil:

> I form the light and create darkness, I bring prosperity and create disaster; I, YHWH, do all these things... (Isaiah 45:7)

However this is quite different from the claim that God is the author of moral evil, perversity and rebellion.

The Indwelling God

The second distinction between YHWH and Allah is that YHWH, the God of the Bible, makes himself present in creation, in time and space, and in human affairs.

Examples from the Hebrew Scriptures:

> …the Spirit of God was hovering over the waters. (Genesis 1:2)

> Then the man and his wife heard the sound of YHWH God as he was walking in the garden in the cool of the day, and they hid from YHWH God among the trees of the garden. (Genesis 3:8)

> YHWH appeared to Abraham near the great trees of Mamre while he was sitting at the entrance to his tent in the heat of the day. (Genesis 18:1)

> But Moses said to God, "Who am I, that I should go to Pharaoh and bring the Israelites out of Egypt?" And God said, "I will be with you." (Exodus 3:11–12)

*By day YHWH went ahead of them in a pillar of cloud
to guide them on their way and by night in a pillar of
fire to give them light, so that they could travel by
day or night.* (Exodus 13:21)

*Place the cover on top of the ark and put in the ark
the Testimony, which I will give you. There, above
the cover between the two cherubim that are over
the ark of the Testimony, I will meet with you and
give you all my commands for the Israelites.* (Exodus
25:21–22)

*YHWH replied, "My Presence will go with you, and I
will give you rest." Then Moses said to him, "If your
Presence does not go with us, do not send us up
from here."* (Exodus 33:14–15)

*When the priests withdrew from the Holy Place, the
cloud filled the temple of YHWH. And the priests
could not perform their service because of the
cloud, for the glory of YHWH filled his temple. Then
Solomon said, "YHWH has said that he would dwell
in a dark cloud; I have indeed built a magnificent
temple for you, a place for you to dwell forever."*
(1 Kings 8:10–13)

*YHWH is in his holy temple; YHWH is on his heavenly
throne. He observes the sons of men; his eyes
examine them.* (Psalm 11:4)

*Do not cast me from your presence or take your
Holy Spirit from me.* (Psalm 51:11)

*Then you will know that I am in Israel, that I am
YHWH your God, and that there is no other; never
again will my people be shamed. "And afterward, I
will pour out my Spirit on all people. Your sons and
daughters will prophesy, your old men will dream
dreams, your young men will see visions. Even on
my servants, both men and women, I will pour out
my Spirit in those days."* (Joel 2:27–29)

But YHWH is in his holy temple; let all the earth be silent before him. (Habakkuk 2:20)

YHWH your God is with you [lit. 'in the midst of you'], *he is mighty to save.* (Zephaniah 3:17)

Examples from the New Testament:

The virgin will be with child and will give birth to a son, and they will call him Immanuel – which means, "God with us." (Matthew 1:23)

[Jesus to his disciples:] " *...teaching them to obey everything I have commanded you. And surely I am with you always, to the very end of the age."* (Matthew 28:20)

He was in the world, and though the world was made through him, the world did not recognize him. (John 1:10)

Jesus replied, "If anyone loves me, he will obey my teaching. My Father will love him, and we will come to him and make our home with him." (John 14:23)

All of them were filled with the Holy Spirit and began to speak in other tongues as the Spirit enabled them. (Acts 2:4)

You, however, are controlled not by the sinful nature but by the Spirit, if the Spirit of God lives in you. And if anyone does not have the Spirit of Christ, he does not belong to Christ. (Romans 8:9)

For in Christ all the fullness of the Deity lives in bodily form... (Colossians 2:9)

If anyone acknowledges that Jesus is the Son of God, God lives in him and he in God. (1 John 4:15)

And I heard a loud voice from the throne saying, "Now the dwelling of God is with men, and he will live with them. They will be his people, and God himself will be with them and be their God. He will wipe every tear from their eyes. There will be no more death or mourning or crying or pain, for the old order of things has passed away." (Revelation 21:3–4)

The presence of God is crucial in a Biblical theology of:

- Christology – God present to us as Jesus the Messiah

- The Holy Spirit – the powerful presence of God

- The Trinity – God with us through his Son and his Spirit

- The Church – the people of God, the 'Body of Christ', constituted by God's saving presence

- The Kingdom of God – established through the coming of God

- Salvation – God saves by 'visiting' his people

The idea of a transcendent, creator God making himself present in human affairs may present us with some philosophical puzzles. Nevertheless, according to the Bible, being distinctively present in time and space, and even in human beings, is not beyond God's capacities.

In Islam Allah is never specifically or distinctively present in time, space or human affairs. The conception of Allah is too transcendent for this. The Quran, unlike the Bible, does not speak of Allah as coming near or indwelling anything. As Ahmad ibn Naqib al-Misri put it:

> He is not delimited by magnitude, contained by place, encompassed by directions, or bounded by heavens or earth. ... He does not indwell in anything, nor anything indwell in Him. He is as exalted above containment in space as He is above confinement in time.[34]

34   Keller (trans.), *The Reliance of the Traveller*, vol.1.3, pp.817–818; my emphasis.

At the same time, Ibn Naqib points out that Allah is omnipresent, being everywhere at once, although nowhere in particular. He is distant from everything, but close to everything at the same time, and his nearness is completely unlike the nearness of objects to each other:

> He is above the Throne, the heavens, and all else to the farthest reaches of the stars, with an aboveness that does not increase His nearness to the Throne or heavens, or His distance from the earth and what lies beneath it. He is as exalted in degree above the Throne and the heavens as He is above the earth and its depths, though He is near to everything in existence, nearer to a servant than his own jugular vein, and is witness to everything. His nearness no more resembles the nearness of objects to one another than His entity resembles the entities of objects.[35]

> _____
> The Quran, unlike the Bible, does not speak of Allah as coming near or indwelling anything.
> _____

There are a number of verses in the Quran which underpin these perspectives:

> *To Allah belong the East and the West; whithersoever you turn, there is the Face of Allah; Allah is All-embracing, All-knowing.* (Q2:109)

> *And when My servants question thee concerning Me – I am near to answer the call of the call, when he calls to Me; so let them respond to Me, and let them believe in Me; haply so they will go aright.* (Q2:180–184)

---

35   Keller (trans.), *The Reliance of the Traveller*, vol.1.3, pp.817–818.

To Allah belongs all that is in the heavens and in the earth, and Allah encompasses everything. (Q4:125)

We [Allah] are nearer to him [human beings] than the jugular vein. (Q50:15–19)

And a tradition which says that Allah is 'very near':

Narrated Abu Musa:

We were with the Prophet on a journey, and whenever we ascended a high place, we used to say, "Allahu Akbar." The Prophet said, "Don't trouble yourselves too much! You are not calling a deaf or an absent person, but you are calling One Who Hears, Sees, and is very near." ... He said, to me, "O 'Abdullah bin Qais! Say, 'La hawla wala quwwata illa billah', for it is a treasure of the treasures of Paradise."[36]

In this hadith, to refer to Allah as 'near' simply means that he is cognizant of us and our actions whenever and wherever we may be. This Islamic concept of Allah being 'very near' is not meant to mean a time-specific or place-specific presence. Allah can never draw near to a place, or leave it, or be closer to one person than other. He is never present today but absent tomorrow. It also would be impossible for anyone to 'draw near' to Allah. His nearness is just a way of speaking about his omniscience and omnipotence, not of actual presence.

This characteristic of Islamic faith has many consequences. As we have seen, the Quran has no conception of the Holy Spirit as the presence of God with people.

Let us consider two consequences of this difference between the Bible and Islam relating to the understanding of God's purposes on earth, and the understanding of heaven.

36   *Sahih Al-Bukhari*, vol.9, 7386.

The 'Kingdom of God' as a sharia state

The Quran does not conceive of relationship with Allah in terms of the presence of Allah, but in terms of obedience to his commands. This makes his follower a 'slave of Allah' (an *Abdullah*). Obedience is realized in the *Dar al-Islam*, the 'house of Islam', not the place where Allah dwells, but the zone wherein Islam is dominant and human beings implement sharia law. The eschatological hope of Islam is that this zone will expand to include all the earth in a politically-realized sharia state. This is referred to as the 'Kingdom of Allah'.

In the Christian faith, the phrase 'Kingdom of God' is used, but with a completely different meaning. This is not understood in terms of a political Kingdom, but in terms of the saving presence of God in human affairs. Jesus' announcement that 'the Kingdom of God is at hand' was demonstrated by his work of healing the sick and in overcoming the power of sin and evil to control and destroy human lives, not through establishing a political system:

> *Jesus went into Galilee, proclaiming the good news of God. "The time has come," he said. "The kingdom of God is near. Repent and believe the good news!"* (Mark 1:14–15)

> *Jesus went throughout Galilee, teaching in their synagogues, preaching the good news of the kingdom, and healing every disease and sickness among the people.* (Matthew 4:23)

> *But if I drive out demons by the finger of God, then the kingdom of God has come to you.* (Luke 11:20)

Jesus sent out his twelve apostles (*apostle* literally means 'sent one'), and gave them the same task of announcing and demonstrating the Kingdom of God:

When Jesus had called the Twelve together, he gave them power and authority to drive out all demons and to cure diseases, and he sent them out to preach the kingdom of God and to heal the sick. (Luke 9:1–2)

[Jesus commanded them:] *"When you enter a town and are welcomed, eat what is set before you. Heal the sick who are there and tell them, 'The kingdom of God is near you.'"* (Luke 10:8–9)

Jesus explicitly rejected the idea that this Kingdom was a political entity, or a geographical territory:

Once, having been asked by the Pharisees when the kingdom of God would come, Jesus replied, "The kingdom of God does not come with your careful observation, nor will people say, 'Here it is,' or 'There it is,' because the kingdom of God is within [or 'among'] you." (Luke 17:20–21)

> In Christian theology the 'wow' factor in heaven is all about being in God's presence.

Jesus also made a distinction between things which are God's, and things which belong to Caesar, thus allowing for a distinct secular domain within Christian theology:

"Is it right to pay taxes to Caesar or not? Should we pay or shouldn't we?" But Jesus knew their hypocrisy. "Why are you trying to trap me?" he asked. "Bring me a denarius and let me look at it." They brought the coin, and he asked them, "Whose portrait is this? And whose inscription?" "Caesar's," they replied. Then Jesus said to them, "Give to Caesar what is Caesar's and to God what is God's." (Mark 12:14–17)

According to the Biblical world view, the people of God, who enjoy his presence, are themselves exiles in this world – 'aliens and strangers' as 1 Peter 2:11 puts it.

In Islam, however, the world itself becomes domain for faithful Muslims to impose the sovereignty of Allah. There is no distinction between secular and sacred, or between church and state. Far from being strangers in the world, 'the earth belongs to Allah and his Apostle',[37] so the whole world rightfully belongs to Allah, and, many would say, to his representatives, the Muslim community.

The hope of Heaven is not the same in Christianity and Islam

In Christian theology the 'wow' factor in heaven is all about being in God's presence (Revelation 21:3–4). Although mentioned in a hadith and the Quran, Allah's presence is not centre-stage in the Islamic vision of paradise. Instead most Islamic references to paradise focus on the theme of eternal success: there will an absence of stress and trouble, many great delights and pleasures, including, according to many authorities and the Quran itself, sexual partners. This is the 'oasis' view of heaven.

---

37   Muhammad gave this charge to the Jews of Medina: "O ye assembly of Jews, accept Islam (and) you will be safe. [And after repeating this another two times, he said:] You should know that the earth belongs to Allah and His Apostle, and I wish that I should expel you from this land. Those of you who have any property with them should sell it, otherwise they should know that the earth belongs to Allah and His Apostle (and they may have to go away leaving everything behind)." (*Sahih Muslim*, vol.3, 4363)

YHWH is Holy

It is in the understanding of the holiness of God that we find one the most striking differences between YHWH and Allah. Any dictionary or encyclopedia of the Bible will include a long entry on holiness, with discussion of the holiness of God. Yet it is a remarkable fact that McAuliffe's *Encyclopedia of the Qur'an* (2001–2004), which reflects the very latest scholarship in Quran research, includes no entry for *holy* or *holiness*.

The internet encyclopedia *Wikipedia* includes extensive articles and references on points of Islamic theology: for example the entries on *Jesus*, *sin* and *creation* include Islamic sections. However, as at April 2006, Wikipedia's entry on *holiness* included no reference to Islam.

Holiness in the Bible

Holiness seems an unimportant, almost incidental, concept in Islam, whilst in both Judaism and Christianity it is absolutely centre-stage. In the Bible, YHWH is above all holy and, what is more, God's people are called to be holy in order to be like him:

> *YHWH said to Moses, "Speak to the entire assembly of Israel and say to them: 'Be holy because I, YHWH your God, am holy.'"* (Leviticus 19:1–2)

To approach God is to encounter his holiness:

> *'Among those who approach me I will show myself holy; in the sight of all the people I will be honored.'* (Leviticus 10:3)

Holiness functions in the Bible as a conceptual bridge which explains what it means to approach God and come into his presence. The 'most holy' place was the space where God dwells, enthroned above the Ark of the covenant, and the 'holy place' was separated off from this by a curtain:

> *Hang the curtain from the clasps and place the ark of the Testimony behind the curtain. The curtain will separate the Holy Place from the Most Holy Place. Put the atonement cover on the ark of the Testimony in the Most Holy Place.* (Exodus 33–34)

Notice that the closer one moves to the presence of God, the more the holiness increases.

The famous story of Moses and the burning bush makes clear this link between God's presence and holiness. The ground was holy, because God was present in that place:

> *When YHWH saw that he had gone over to look, God called to him from within the bush, "Moses! Moses!" And Moses said, "Here I am." "Do not come any closer," God said. "Take off your sandals, for the place where you are standing is holy ground." Then he said, "I am the God of your father, the God of Abraham, the God of Isaac and the God of Jacob." At this, Moses hid his face, because he was afraid to look at God.* (Exodus 3:4–6)

Later, Mount Sinai was to be made off limits to the people of Israel as holy (Exodus 19:23) because God's presence was dwelling on its heights. Then later, when the temple was established, it was holy as the dwelling place for God, and the city surrounding it was also designated as holy:

> *The LORD is in his holy temple; the LORD is on his heavenly throne.* (Psalm 11:4)

> *...the city of God, the holy place where the Most High dwells.* (Psalm 46:4)

The Spirit of YHWH is by his very nature holy – as the Spirit of YHWH is the living presence of God. To encounter this presence is to engage with God's holiness, hence the appropriateness of the title 'Holy Spirit'.

> When we carefully study the Quran, and compare it to the Bible, we can conclude that the concept of the holiness of Allah is not central in Islam.

The saving work of God causes his people to be consecrated or sanctified, that is, to 'be made or become holy':

> *Then you will remember to obey all my commands and will be consecrated* [lit. 'be holy'] *to your God. I am YHWH your God, who brought you out of Egypt to be your God. I am YHWH your God.* (Numbers 15:40)

Holiness in Islam

In contrast to the hundreds of references to the holiness of YHWH in the Bible, in the Quran Allah is referred to as holy only twice. *Al-Quddus* ('the Holy') is listed among

Islam's ninety-nine Beautiful Names of Allah, but forty-six of the ninety-nine names appear more frequently in the Quran than *Al-Quddus*.

The things that are more usually termed 'holy' in the Quran and hadiths are land, battles, certain times, and the Quran itself. This reflects the idea that certain objects or places are sacred, being set apart for a religious purpose. This understanding underpins the significance in Islam of 'sacred sites' such as Mecca and Medina.

What is striking about the Quran's references to holy objects and places is that they are not connected to a fundamental conception of Allah's inherent holiness, or his indwelling presence, such as is found in the Bible. Mecca is holy to Muslims, not because Allah is holy and Allah dwells in Mecca, but because by divine decree Mecca has been set aside to be a place of devotion and religious observance for Islam.

When we carefully study the Quran, and compare it to the Bible, we can conclude that the concept of the holiness of Allah is not central in Islam. Holiness is not one of the governing ideas of Islam defining the very nature of Allah, and it is marginal to the core concerns of Islamic doctrine. If every reference to holiness was removed from the Quran, the Islamic faith would be barely touched, but if the same were to be done with the Bible, it would be absolutely gutted.

In the Bible, the people of God are called *saints*, an expression which means 'holy ones', dedicated and consecrated to YHWH. In contrast, in Islam believers are known as *Muslims*, which means 'submitters'.

There is an important difference between holiness and submission. In Islam submission is not an attribute of Allah, but only of his slaves. Human submission is matched by Allah's dominance. In Biblical faith, however, human holiness is a way of participating in God's own holy nature. The concept of submission emphasizes the otherness of God from humanity, the concept of holiness emphasizes God's identification with his creatures: 'You shall be holy, for I YHWH your God am holy.' (Leviticus 19:2, a call renewed in 1 Peter 1:13–16)

In His Image

The fact that people are invited by God to share his attribute of holiness opens up the question of how created humanity can partake in the attributes of God. To understand this we need to consider the Bible's teaching on the 'image of God'.

> *Then God said, "Let us make man in our image, in our likeness, and let them rule over the fish of the sea and the birds of the air, over the livestock, over all the earth, and over all the creatures that move along the ground." So God created man in his own image, in the image of God he created him; male and female he created them.* (Genesis 1:26–27)

The doctrine of humans being created in the image of God has profound implications.

It means that anthropomorphic language can be used about God. Some examples are: God as the jilted husband in Hosea, God as Father of Israel in Exodus (Exodus 4:22–23), and also in the self-awareness of Jesus. Similarly expressions such as 'the hand of the Lord' are used freely:

The Lord's hand was with them, and a great number of people believed and turned to the Lord. (Acts 11:21)

The sin of shirk ('association')

Islam does use anthropomorphic language about Allah. For example, in the Quran Allah is said to 'see' things. However the use of such expressions is much less extensive than in the Bible and Christian thought. Nevertheless, there is a hadith which states that man was made in Allah's image:

> *Narrated Abu Huraira:*
>
> *The Prophet said, "Allah created Adam in his image, sixty cubits (about 30 metres) in height. When He created him, He said (to him), 'Go and greet that group of angels sitting there, and listen what they will say in reply to you, for that will be your greeting and the greeting of your offspring.' Adam (went and) said, 'As-Salamu 'alaikum (Peace be upon you).' They replied, 'As-Salamu 'alaika wa Rahmatullah (peace and Allah's Mercy be on you).'...The Prophet added, "So whoever will enter Paradise, will be of the shape and picture of Adam. Since then the creation of Adam's (offspring) (i.e. stature of human beings) is being diminished continuously up to the present time."*[38]

Muhammad Muhsin Khan, the translator of the *Sahih Bukhari*, felt it necessary to clarify this hadith with an unusually long footnote. He explains that the 'image' has a linguistic meaning: that while the same words are used to describe attributes of Adam and Allah – such as *life* and *knowledge* – these mean different things, and the attributes of Adam and Allah are not to be compared:

38   *Sahih Bukhari*, vol.8, 6227.

'His Image' means that Adam has been bestowed with life, knowledge, power of hearing, seeing, understanding, etc., but the features of Adam are different from those of Allah, only the names are the same, e.g. Allah has life and knowledge and power of understanding, and Adam also has them, but there is no comparison between the Creator and the created thing.[39]

Why is this disclaimer required? It is necessary because this hadith is a theological oddity, which is not consistent with and cannot override the clear teachings of the Quran.

According to the Quran, the idea that people should be like Allah, or seek to become like him in any way, is regarded as blasphemy. Allah is incomparable, wholly one, unique, and apart:

> Say: 'He is Allah, One, Allah, the Everlasting Refuge, who has not begotten, and has not been begotten, and equal to Him is not any one.' (Q112)

Shirk ('association') is the name given for the sin of associating or joining anything or anyone with Allah. Literally meaning 'sharing' or 'division', shirk is the vice which is in opposition to tawhid ('unification'), the doctrine of Allah's unity. In the Quran, pagan polytheism and Christian Trinitarian doctrines are both rejected as examples of shirk.

In the Quran shirk is referred to as the worst and only unforgivable sin. All other sins Allah may forgive if he chooses, but not this:

> Allah forgives not that aught should be with Him associated; less than that He forgives to whomsoever He will. Whoso associates with Allah anything, has indeed forged a mighty sin. (Q4:50–54)

---

39   Sahih Bukhari, vol.8. p.138, fn.1.

In Islamic theology *shirk* can also mean describing others as comparable with Allah, or acting as if others were comparable to Allah or enjoyed any of the rights or attributes of Allah. In Islam's critique of pagan religion, not only is the belief that there are multiple gods a form of *shirk*, but the practice of worshipping an idol as god is also *shirk*. *Shirk* can also include attributing human qualities to Allah, or godlike qualities to humans. It could also include worshipping Allah for the wrong reasons, such as for self-interest, because that would set your own desires up as an object of worship.

Biblical implications of the 'image of God'

In contrast to the doctrine of *shirk*, the Biblical doctrine of God means that the character of God is regarded as a model or example for people to follow. For example, the experience of grace is meant to make us gracious, like God:

> *Dear friends, since God so loved us, we also ought to love one another. No one has ever seen God; but if we love one another, God lives in us and his love is made complete in us.* (1 John 4:11–12)

The Biblical perspective that believers are 'children of God' implies that the children should be like their parent: as God is, so his children should be:

> *Be imitators of God, therefore, as dearly loved children and live a life of love, just as Christ loved us and gave himself up for us as a fragrant offering and sacrifice to God.* (Ephesians 5:1–2)

In Christian thought the imitation of God finds its clearest focus in Jesus, who is the object, but also the goal of faith. The Christian's destiny is to be like Jesus Christ:

Dear friends, now we are children of God, and what we will be has not yet been made known. But we know that when he appears, we shall be like him, for we shall see him as he is. (1 John 3:2)

And we, who with unveiled faces all reflect the Lord's glory, are being transformed into his likeness with ever-increasing glory, which comes from the Lord, who is the Spirit. (2 Corinthians 3:18)

This idea is elaborated in the New Testament in the language of being conformed to the pattern of Christ's life – as God incarnate – in his death, resurrection, glory, and ultimately also his reign:

Therefore I endure everything for the sake of the elect, that they too may obtain the salvation that is in Christ Jesus, with eternal glory. This a trustworthy saying: If we died with him, we will also live with him; if we endure, we will also reign with him. (2 Timothy 2:10–12)

There are many outworkings of the contrasting doctrines of the 'image of God' in Christianity, and 'association' in Islam. We shall here focus on just two domains of application: the ethics of conflict, and politics.

> In Christian thought the imitation of God finds its clearest focus in Jesus.

Ethical implications: conflict

The important practical implications of these different understandings of the nature of YHWH and Allah can be seen in the teachings of the Bible and the Quran on attitudes to enemies and to suffering.

Jesus commands his followers to love their enemies, because if they do this they will be like God, 'children of your Father in heaven':

> *You have heard that it was said, 'Love your neighbor and hate your enemy.' But I tell you: Love your enemies and pray for those who persecute you, that you may be sons of your Father in heaven. He causes his sun to rise on the evil and the good, and sends rain on the righteous and the unrighteous.* (Matthew 5:43–45)

Paul elaborates this theme in Romans, forbidding revenge and cursing, even of enemies:

> *Bless those who persecute you; bless and do not curse. Rejoice with those who rejoice; mourn with those who mourn. Live in harmony with one another. Do not be proud, but be willing to associate with people of low position. Do not be conceited. Do not repay anyone evil for evil. Be careful to do what is right in the eyes of everybody. If it is possible, as far as it depends on you, live at peace with everyone. Do not take revenge, my friends, but leave room for God's wrath, for it is written: "It is mine to avenge; I will repay," says the Lord. On the contrary: "If your enemy is hungry, feed him; if he is thirsty, give him something to drink. In doing this, you will heap burning coals* [metaphorically, not literally] *on his head." Do not be overcome by evil, but overcome evil with good.* (Romans 12:14–21)

The apostle Peter instructs Christians not to return abuse, nor to threaten those who cause Christians to suffer. Why would he give such instructions? If they achieve this, Peter says, they will be following God's example shown to them in Christ:

But if you suffer for doing good and you endure it, this is commendable before God. To this you were called, because Christ suffered for you, leaving you an example, that you should follow in his steps. "He committed no sin, and no deceit was found in his mouth." When they hurled their insults at him, he did not retaliate; when he suffered, he made no threats. Instead, he entrusted himself to him who judges justly. He himself bore our sins in his body on the tree, so that we might die to sins and live for righteousness; by his wounds you have been healed. (1 Peter 2:20–24)

The attitude of Islam to enemies, expressed in many Quranic verses and hadiths, and in countless statements by theologians and especially in textbooks dealing with the doctrines of jihad, is quite the opposite. It is the right and duty of Muslims to be strict in exacting retribution against their enemies, who are also the enemies of Allah:

And fight in the way of Allah with those who fight with you, but aggress not: Allah loves not the aggressors. And slay them wherever you come upon them, and expel them from where they expelled you; persecution [of believers] is more grievous than slaying [of unbelievers]. ... Fight them, till there is no persecution and the religion is Allah's; ... Whoso commits aggression against you, do you commit aggression against him like as he has committed against you; and fear you Allah, and know that Allah is with the godfearing. (Q2:185–189)

O believers, take not for your intimates outside yourselves; such men spare nothing to ruin you; they yearn for you to suffer. Hatred has already shown itself of their mouths, and what their breasts conceal is yet greater. Now We have made clear to you the signs, if you understand. Ha, there you are; you love them, and they love you not; you believe in the

Book, all of it, and when they meet you they say, 'We believe,' but when they go privily, they bite at you their fingers, enraged. Say: 'Die in your rage; Allah knows the thoughts in the breasts.' (Q3:110–119)

O believers, take not My enemy and your enemy for friends, offering them love, though they have disbelieved in the truth that has come to you, expelling the Messenger and you because you believe in Allah your Lord. If you go forth to struggle in My way and seek My good pleasure, secretly loving them, yet I know very well what you conceal and what you publish; and whosoever of you does that, has gone astray from the right way. (Q60:1–4)

The following passage instructs Muslims that they are not forbidden to show kindness and fairness to non-Muslims who are at peace with them, but they are forbidden to make friends with those who have fought against them.

Allah forbids you not, as regards those who have not fought you in religion's cause, nor expelled you from your habitations, that you should be kindly to them, and act justly towards them; surely God loves the just. Allah only forbids you as to those who have fought you in religion's cause, and expelled you from your habitations, and have supported in your expulsion, that you should take them for friends. And whosoever takes them for friends, those – they are the evildoers. (Q60:5–9)

The Quran cites Ibrahim (Abraham) as an exemplary model of enmity towards those who refuse to accept Islam:

You have had a good example in Ibrahim, and those with him, when they said to their people, 'We are quit of you and that you serve, apart from Allah. We disbelieve in you, and between us and you enmity has shown itself, and hatred for ever, until you believe in Allah alone.' (Q60:1–4)

The principle of retribution was not merely a theoretical one for Muhammad. It was lived out by Muhammad through the genocide of the Quraiza Jews of Medina. Muhammad had found this tribe guilty of not coming to the aid of the Muslims when they were besieged by the Meccans. After the Meccans lifted their siege, Muhammad attacked the Quraiza Jews. A hadith from the *Sahih Muslim* reported the outcome of their appeal for clemency:

> *Then he* [Muhammad] *killed their men, and distributed their women, children and properties among the Muslims...*[40]

All adult male Quraiza Jews – six to eight hundred in all – were beheaded in the market place of Medina in a single day, and the women and children were distributed to the Muslims as booty and some Muhammad sold as slaves to purchase weapons for jihad. A few who converted to Islam were permitted to retain their freedom.

The Quran refers to this event as follows:

> *And He brought down those of the People of the Book who supported them from their fortresses and cast terror in their hearts; some you slew, some you made captive. And He bequeathed upon you their lands, their habitations, and their possessions, and a land you never trod. Allah is powerful over everything.* (Q33:25–29)

Islamic authorities who justify this event do so by emphasizing the culpability of the Quraiza Jews. In other words they appeal to the principle of retribution.

These considerations point to a potential inconsistency in Islamic theology. Whilst Islam forbids the imitation of Allah, it does seem that the character of Allah revealed in the Quran exerts an influence upon Muslims' understandings of what is right and wrong in human relationships. In

---

40   *Sahih Muslim*, vol.3, 4364.

this case, Muslims' expected attitude to their enemies is the same attitude shown by Allah to his enemies. In this sense, Muslims are fashioned by the Quran into the image of Allah.

Political implications: the sharia state

The doctrine of *shirk* also applies in the political domain. To submit to any legal or political authority in this world which is not Allah's is also *shirk*:

> And say: 'Praise belongs to Allah, who has not taken to Him a son, and who has not any associate in the Kingdom...' (Q17:100–114)

> They have no protector, apart from Him, and He associates in His government no one. (Q18:25–29)

> Judgment belongs only to Allah; He has commanded that you shall not serve any but Him. That is the right religion; but most men know not. (Q12:35–39)

This teaching underpins the radical Islamists' desire to overthrow democratic states and replace them with sharia rule. According to some extreme formulations, any political authority which is not based on sharia law is a form of idolatry. Democracy has even been called a 'satanic religion'.[41] Although many Muslims reject such extreme views, it has been the classic view of Islamic jurists that a government which does not submit to sharia principles is invalid. It is because of this that the constitutions of so many majority Muslim nations name the sharia as the source of all legislation.

In contrast, the Christian desire to conform to God's purposes is conceptualised as a process of transformation to become more like God in Christ. Although this goal of transformation can be applied to the political process, it need not require a political implementation, and a Christian

41   *Democracy is a religion*; www.iisna.com/articles/democracy.htm

community which has no access to political power can still pursue it with integrity.

It is important to note in this context that there was no expectation of Christendom in the New Testament. Quite the contrary. The Christian hope of participation in God's nature – in the image of God restored – does not have political realization as one of its preconditions. The exercise of political rule may be ordered by God, but it need not be Christian to be respected and obeyed. Paul, writing to Christians in Rome, who were not strangers to persecution at the hands of the authorities, had this to say about respecting the pagan Roman emperor:

> *Everyone must submit himself to the governing authorities, for there is no authority except that which God has established. The authorities that exist have been established by God. Consequently, he who rebels against the authority is rebelling against what God has instituted, and those who do so will bring judgment on themselves. For rulers hold no terror for those who do right, but for those who do wrong. Do you want to be free from fear of the one in authority? Then do what is right and he will commend you. For he is God's servant to do you good. But if you do wrong, be afraid, for he does not bear the sword for nothing. He is God's servant, an agent of wrath to bring punishment on the wrongdoer. Therefore, it is necessary to submit to the authorities, not only because of possible punishment but also because of conscience. This is also why you pay taxes, for the authorities are God's servants, who give their full time to governing. Give everyone what you owe him: If you owe taxes, pay taxes; if revenue, then revenue; if respect, then respect; if honor, then honor.* (Romans 13:1–7)

Building on these theological foundations, for the first three centuries Christians had no political power until the edict of Milan in AD 312, when Constantine officially tolerated Christianity, and AD 380 when, under Theodosius, Christiaity became the state religion.

Even when Christendom was instituted, the distinction between the 'ecclesiastical' and 'secular' domains was recognized from the beginning, and it became deeply embedded in the terminologies of Christian cultures. It was reflected, for example, in the difference between medieval secular and ecclesiastical courts. However there is not even the language in classical Islamic Arabic thought to translate the distinction between 'secular' and 'ecclesiastical'.

Down the centuries, very many Christian communities have existed outside of a 'Christendom' framework including, for example, the English non-conformist protestant tradition, the present-day Christians of China, and the formerly populous Christian communities who continued on after Islamic conquest. Christians who still live under Islamic rule continue to maintain their hope in the Kingdom of God, but without harbouring aspirations of political dominance over their Islamic neighbours.

In contrast, among Muslim minorities which have sprung up throughout the former lands of 'Christendom' there are always to be found some whose faith is sustained by the vision that, one day, Islam will be politically dominant in their new homeland. In numerous sermons and tracts and on numerous websites they explain this hope as the application to the political domain of the doctrine of 'association': Allah will tolerate no associates in his reign over the earth.

Who Does God Love?

In the Torah, when Moses asks to see God's face, God reveals instead his character to him, specifically his faithful love:

> Then YHWH came down in the cloud and stood there with him and proclaimed his name, YHWH. And he passed in front of Moses, proclaiming, "YHWH, YHWH, the compassionate and gracious God, slow to anger, abounding in love and faithfulness, maintaining love to thousands, and forgiving wickedness, rebellion and sin. Yet he does not leave the guilty unpunished; he punishes the children and their children for the sin of the fathers to the third and fourth generation." (Exodus 34:5–7)

This famous passage contrasts God's judgment, which extends for a few generations, with his forgiveness and faithfulness reaching to the 'thousandth generation'.

Hebrew *hesed* ('loving kindness') is not an emotion, but a covenantal commitment.

This characteristic of God – his faithfulness in love to those to whom he has covenanted himself – is revealed again and again throughout the Bible. A powerful image is given when the prophet Hosea is told to marry a prostitute and be faithful to her. This is the way, he is told, that God relates to his people Israel:

> *I will betroth you to me forever; I will betroth you in righteousness and justice, in love and compassion. I will betroth you in faithfulness, and you will acknowledge YHWH.* (Hosea 2:19–20)

The idea of Allah deliberately comparing himself to the husband of a prostitute, as a way of describing how great his love is, would be unthinkable in Islam.

Perfect prophets or agents of grace?

In Islamic tradition prophets are regarded as exemplary, having a superior character. Otherwise, it is thought, Allah would not have accepted to use them.

On the other hand, prophets, patriarchs and kings of the Bible are all very imperfect, being instruments of God's grace. Most prophets are portrayed as sinners. Daniel is a rare exception, yet even he concedes his sinfulness to God (Daniel 9:20).

This distinction provides interesting opportunities in interfaith dialogue, as when Muslims read the Bible they can find the transgressions of the 'Islamic prophets' to be quite surprising: David was an adulterer and a murderer; Abraham married his half-sister and in two foreign situations lied implying that they were not married but that she was his sister; Lot committed incest with his daughters while drunk; and Solomon erected temples to pagan idols, including to Molech, the god of child sacrifice.

God loves sinners

When the Bible says that God's love is everlasting, this is in spite of human sinfulness.

There are a number of points in the Bible, which state that God hates sin and condemns those who sin. For example:

> You must not live according to the customs of the nations I am going to drive out before you. Because they did all these things, I abhorred them. (Leviticus 20:23)

We also read that God has a special love for those who obey and follow him:

> Whoever has my commands and obeys them, he is the one who loves me. He who loves me will be loved by my Father and I will love him and show myself to him. (John 14:21)

> No, the Father himself loves you because you have loved me and have believed that I came from God. (John 16:27)

However this is also balanced by YHWH's favour and love, given to those who do not deserve it. This is the 'good news' of Jesus Christ, which is introduced in the Old Testament in God's love for Israel, and revealed more clearly in the New Testament. It is this love which gives humans hope in the face of the reality of judgment.

> YHWH appeared to us in the past, saying: "I have loved you with an everlasting love; I have drawn you with loving-kindness." (Jeremiah 31:3)

> For men are not cast off by the Lord forever. Though he brings grief, he will show compassion, so great is his unfailing love. For he does not willingly bring affliction or grief to the children of men. (Lamentations 3:31–33)

> For God so loved the world that he gave his one and only Son, that whoever believes in him shall not perish but have eternal life. For God did not send

his Son into the world to condemn the world, but to save the world through him. (John 3:16–17)

But because of his great love for us, God, who is rich in mercy, made us alive with Christ even when we were dead in transgressions – it is by grace you have been saved. (Ephesians 2:4–5)

You see, at just the right time, when we were still powerless, Christ died for the ungodly. Very rarely will anyone die for a righteous man, though for a good man someone might possibly dare to die. But God demonstrates his own love for us in this: While we were still sinners, Christ died for us. (Romans 5:6–8)

This is love: not that we loved God, but that he loved us and sent his Son as an atoning sacrifice for our sins. (1 John 4:10)

We love because he first loved us. (1 John 4:19)

This is so unlike Allah of the Quran. In the Quran, Allah loves, protects and shows mercy to those who follow his commands, who fight in his cause in battle, and who love Allah. But much more frequent than statements about who Allah loves are statements about who Allah does not love: transgressors, ungrateful people, those who do mischief, traitors, and those who go beyond Allah's limits.

These dynamics are summed up in this pair of verses:

Say: 'If you love Allah, follow me [Muhammad], and Allah will love you, and forgive you your sins; Allah is All-forgiving, All-compassionate.'

Say: 'Obey Allah and the Messenger.' But if they turn their backs, Allah loves not the unbelievers. (Q3:25–29)

On Allah's love:

Nay, but whoso fulfils his covenant and fears Allah, Allah loves the godfearing. (Q3:70)

Many a Prophet there has been, with whom thousands manifold have fought, and they fainted not for what smote them in Allah's way, neither weakened, nor did they humble themselves; and Allah loves the patient. ...

And Allah gave them the reward of this world and the fairest reward of the world to come; and Allah loves the good-doers. (Q3:140–144)

It was by some mercy of Allah that thou wast gentle to them; hadst thou been harsh and hard of heart,

> The love of Allah of the Quran is conditional. The love of YHWH of the Bible is a gift of grace.

they would have scattered from about thee. So pardon them, and pray forgiveness for them, and take counsel with them in the affair; and when you are resolved, put thy trust in Allah; surely Allah loves those who put their trust [in Him]. (Q3:150–154)

Surely those who believe and do deeds of righteousness – unto them the All-merciful shall assign love. (Q19:95–99)

On Allah's not loving:

But as for the believers, who do deeds of righteousness, He will pay them in full their wages: and Allah loves not the evildoers. (Q3:50)

Assuredly Allah will defend those who believe; surely Allah loves not any ungrateful traitor. (Q22:39)

O believers, forbid not such good things as Allah has permitted you; and transgress not; Allah loves not transgressors. (Q5:89)

The love of Allah of the Quran is conditional. The love of YHWH of the Bible is a gift of grace. The concept of grace as God's faithful love to sinners – 'Amazing grace, how sweet the sound' – is central in the Christian faith, but not in Islam. The closest equivalent in Islam would be Allah's mercy shown to the righteous, that is, to those who submit to him:

Narrated Abu Huraira:

I heard Allah's Apostle saying, "The good deeds of any person will not make him enter Paradise." (i.e., None can enter Paradise through his good deeds.) They (the Prophet's companions) said, 'Not even you, O Allah's Apostle?' He said, "Not even I, unless Allah bestows His Favor and Mercy on me. So be moderate in your religious deeds and do the deeds that are within your ability: and none of you should wish for death, for if he is a gooddoer, he shall increase his good deeds, and if he is an evildoer, he may repent to Allah."[42]

Although the Quran encourages those who obey Allah to hope for his mercy, Islamic theology has always emphasized that if Allah were to punish people this could never be unjust, as he is not obligated to anyone:

He is not obliged to anyone to do anything, nor is injustice on His part conceivable, for He does not owe any rights to anyone.[43]

Yet he rewards those that worship Him for their obedience on account of his promise and beneficence, not of their merit nor of necessity, since there is nothing which He can be tied to perform; nor

---

42   *Sahih Al-Bukhari*, vol.7, 5673.

43   Keller (trans.), *The Reliance of the Traveller*, vol.1.9, p.821.

can any injustice be supposed in Him, nor can He be under any obligation to any person whatsoever. Al-Ghazzali (d.1111)[44]

Nothing is too difficult to him, whether it be the creation of a fly or that of the seven heavens. He receives neither profit nor loss from whatever may happen. If all the Infidels became believers and all the irreligious pious, he would gain no advantage. On the other hand, if all believers became infidels, he would suffer no loss. He can do what he wills, and whatever he wills comes to pass. He is not obliged to act. Imam al-Barqavi (d.1132)[45]

---

44   Hughes, *Dictionary of Islam*, p.141ff.

45   From the *Haft Sifat* of al-Barqavi, as reported in Hughes' *Dictionary of Islam*, pp.144ff.

Is God Faithful?

The faithfulness of YHWH

Throughout the Bible we find that YHWH binds himself into covenants with humanity which are described as eternal, through:

Noah:

"I establish my covenant with you: Never again will all life be cut off by the waters." And God said, "This is the sign of the covenant I am making between me and you and every living creature with you, a covenant for all generations to come…" (Genesis 9:11–12)

Abraham:

"I will establish my covenant as an everlasting covenant between me and you and your descendants after you for the generations to come, to be your God and the God of your descendants after you. The whole land of Canaan, where you are now an alien, I will give as an everlasting possession to you and your descendants after you; and I will be their God." (Genesis 17:7–8)

David:

You said, "I have made a covenant with my chosen one, I have sworn to David my servant, 'I will establish your line forever and make your throne firm through all generations.'" (Psalm 89:3–4)

Jesus:

May the God of peace, who through the blood of the eternal covenant brought back from the dead our Lord Jesus, that great Shepherd of the sheep, equip you with everything good for doing his will, and may he work in us what is pleasing to him, through Jesus Christ, to whom be glory for ever and ever. (Hebrews 13:20–21)

YHWH is unchanging and ever faithful to his word.

YHWH is unchanging and ever faithful to his word. His enduring love towards Israel, not destroying them, but always preserving a remnant, reflects this faithfulness:

God is not a man, that he should lie, nor a son of man, that he should change his mind. Does he speak and then not act? Does he promise and not fulfill? (Numbers 23:19)

Give thanks to YHWH for he is good. His love endures forever. (Psalm 136)

[speaking of the Jews] ...as far as election is concerned, they are loved on account of the patriarchs, for God's gifts and his call are irrevocable. (Romans 11:28–29)

...a faith and knowledge resting on the hope of eternal life, which God, who does not lie, promised before the beginning of time... (Titus 1:2)

Every good and perfect gift is from above, coming down from the Father of the heavenly lights, who does not change like shifting shadows. (James 1:17)

Because God wanted to make the unchanging nature of his purpose very clear to the heirs of what was promised, he confirmed it with an oath. God did this so that, by two unchangeable things in which it is impossible for God to lie, we who have fled to take hold of the hope offered to us may be greatly encouraged. We have this hope as an anchor for the soul, firm and secure. (Hebrews 6:17–19)

At the great covenant renewal ceremony recorded in Deuteronomy, the LORD warns Israel that they will abandon the covenant and become subject to its curses. However this will result in a return to YHWH:

...when you and your children return to YHWH our God and obey him with all your heart and with all your soul according to everything I command you today, then YHWH your God will restore your fortunes and have compassion on you and gather you again from all the nations where he scattered you. Even if you have been banished to the most distant land under the heavens, from there YHWH your God will gather you and bring you back. ... YHWH your God will circumcise your hearts and the hearts of your descendants, so that you may love him with all your heart and with all your soul, and life. (Deuteronomy 30:1–7)

God's faithfulness to a nation which rejects him is not because of any merit on their part, but for the sake of his name:

It is not for your sake, O house of Israel, that I am going to do these things, but for the sake of my holy name... I will show the holiness of my great name... Then the nations will know that I am YHWH...when I show myself holy through you before their eyes. (Ezekiel 36:22–23)

This theme runs through the psalms like a bright golden cord:

For the Lord will not reject his people; he will never forsake his inheritance. (Psalm 94:14–15)

The last book of the Hebrew scriptures, Malachi, includes this statement:

I YHWH do not change. So you, O descendants of Jacob, are not destroyed. (Malachi 3:6)

Faithfulness is not an attribute of Allah

Marmaduke Pickthall's Quran calls Allah the 'best of all schemers', or 'plotters'. The word *makr*, translated by Pickthall as 'scheme' and 'plot', implies making plans with malicious intent:

And they (the disbelievers) schemed, and Allah schemed (against them); and Allah is the best of schemers. (Q3:54, Pickthall's *Koran*)

And when those who disbelieve plot against thee (O Muhammad) to wound thee fatally, or to kill thee, or to bribe thee forth; they plot, but Allah also plotteth; and Allah is the best of plotters. (Q8:30, Pickthall's *Koran*)

Allah acts as he pleases. He is under no obligation to be truthful or fair to human beings:

Allah leads astray whomsoever He will, and he guides whomsoever he will; and he is the All-mighty, the All-wise. (Q14:4)

If We [Allah] had so willed, we could have given every soul its guidance; but My Word is realized – "Assuredly I shall fill Hell with jinn and men all together." (Q32:10–14)

…you are mortals, of His creating; He forgives whom He will, and He chastises whom He will. (Q5:20–25)

In Islam, Allah can also annul or amend previous words that he gave. In Islamic theology this important aspect of Quranic interpretation is known as the principle of 'abrogation':

> Allah acts as he pleases. He is under no obligation to be truthful or fair to human beings.

…we exchange a verse in the place of another verse – and Allah knows well what He is sending down… (Q16:100–104)

And for whatever verse We abrogate or cast into oblivion, We bring a better or the like of it; knowest thou not that Allah is powerful over everything? (Q2:100)

If We willed, We could take away that We have revealed to thee, then thou wouldst find none thereover to guard thee against Us… (Q17:85–89)

This last example refers to a situation where Allah has commanded something. The Quran says that if he subsequently changed his will, the people who were following his earlier instructions would have no defence in pleading their case before him.

A famous example of abrogation was the progressive revelation of the call to jihad. The sequence of revelations, each one correcting or amending the previous one, was summarized by Abdullah bin Muhammad bin Hamid, Sheikh of the Sacred Mosque of Mecca and Chief Justice of Saudi Arabia:

> So at first "the fighting" was forbidden, then it was permitted and after that it as made obligatory – (1) against those who start "the fighting" against you (Muslims) ... (2) and against all those who worship others along with Allah ... as mentioned in Sura Al-Baqra (II), Al'Imran (III), and Ba'arat (IX) ... and other Suras...[46]

Implications for human behaviour

Although in Islam it is forbidden for human beings to seek to be like Allah, the fact that Allah can deceive and arbitrarily change his mind, without this reflecting badly in any way on his justice, is paralleled by the doctrine of *taqiyya*, found in both Sunni and Shiite Islam, which allows and even requires people to lie under certain circumstances:

> ...lying is sometimes permissible, for a given interest, scholars have established criteria defining what types of it are lawful.[47]

The contrast between Islam and Christianity in this respect can be illustrated by comparing what advice these religions give to those who are persecuted for their faith. According to conservative Islamic teachings – both Sunni and Shiite – someone is permitted to lie, and even deny their faith, in order to save themselves. However a Christian should confess Christ even at the cost of their life (Matthew 10:28, 33).

---

46   This essay was included in an earlier edition of Muhammad Muhsin Khan's *Sahih Bukhari* (p.xxiv) and is widely reproduced on the internet.

47   Keller (trans.), *The Reliance of the Traveller*, 'Permissible Lying'. p.745.

A Final Word

There are profound and far-reaching differences in the attributes of YHWH of the Bible and Allah of the Quran. The same is found to apply when one compares Jesus and the Holy Spirit of the Bible with Isa and the Ruh Al-Qudus of the Quran. These differences are deep and significant enough to make it reasonable to reject the claim that Christians and Muslims worship the same God or honour the same Christ.

We can all agree that there are important similarities in the doctrine of God in the two faiths. In both Christianity and Islam, God is creator and final judge, and he works through history to reveal his will to human beings. Islam is founded upon God's rights as creator and his role as giver of guidance to humanity, so that the trajectory of Islamic faith could be said to be:

ISLAM:	PROBLEM	SOLUTION	RESULT
	Ignorance of Allah's laws	Guidance and submission	Success in this life and the next

However what is shared between Christianity and Islam is more than matched by the most profound contrasts in the identity of God, which have far-reaching implications, even affecting attitudes to behavioural ethics, politics and the state.

The Christian hope can be summarized as:

CHRISTIANITY:	PROBLEM	SOLUTION	RESULT
	Sin and alienation	Forgiveness and God's saving presence	Salvation and reconciliation with God

This hope is based upon trust in God's faithful covenantal love, his call to humanity to be restored to their destiny as beings created 'in the image of God', and participation in his life-giving saving presence through Christ and the Holy Spirit. The whole saving potential of the Christian faith is dependent upon attributes of the God of the Bible, including his Trinitarian character, and all these are alien to the nature of Allah of the Quran.

> Islam regards itself as the true Christianity and the true Judaism, so that Allah as he is revealed in the Quran must be the true God of the Christians and Jews.

Furthermore, whilst Islam venerates Jesus, it does so in the guise of Isa, who is an Islamic Christ with only a tenuous connection to the Jesus of history. The job description claimed by Muhammad for the Islamic Christ includes the ultimate destruction of Christianity.

Islam regards itself as the true Christianity and the true Judaism, so that Allah as he is revealed in the Quran must be the true God of the Christians and Jews. Thus the claim that Muslims and Christians worship the same God and honour the same prophets serves the supersessionist program of Islam. To put 'we worship the same God' and 'we reverence your prophets' forward as the basis for interfaith dialogue masks a profound denial of the work of Christ, and rejection of the saving attributes of the God of the Bible. These principles undermine the very foundations of the Christian faith.

If God is as the Quran depicts him, then he has no power to save, not in the way the Christian faith understands salvation. So it is entirely legitimate for Christians to be clear and confident about the witness

> Generally speaking, Muslims who become Christians do not consider themselves to have exchanged gods, but rather to have revised their understanding of Allah.

of the Bible concerning the identity of YHWH, the Lord God of Israel, and to point out to Muslims that the Allah they believe is not the same person as YHWH of the Bible; the Isa they venerate is but a shadow of the true Jesus of Nazareth; and the Ruh Al-Qudus of the Quran is far removed from the one revealed in the Bible as the Holy Spirit of the true and living God.

Grace and thoughtful care is always required when speaking with Muslims. It is important to be informed and aware of the religious sensibilities of others, but not to be bound by them. Generally speaking, Muslims who become Christians do not consider themselves to have exchanged gods, but rather to have revised their understanding of Allah. For this reason it can be helpful for Christians to appeal to and build upon some of the positive understandings of Allah and Isa found in the Quran when presenting their faith to Muslims. However this should be done with discrimination, on the basis of a firm conviction that it is the Bible which truly reveals the identity and character of God, Christ and the Holy Spirit, and not making a hasty and ill-informed surrender to Islam's claim that 'we all worship the same Allah'. The process of welcoming believers into the Christian faith and discipling them also requires a process of getting to know YHWH, and the depth and significance of this task for new Christians believers coming out of Islam should not be underestimated.

Whilst it might appear to the naïve observer to be a principle of unity and co-operative 'co-existence' for the two faiths to 'share' the same God, in fact such a claim papers over deep theological differences. It is essential to acknowledge these differences if Christianity and Islam are to engage constructively with each other in one world. It is also essential for Christians to keep the distinctives of their own faith firmly in mind if they are to retain their theological integrity in dialogue with Muslims. At the same time, few things will equip a Christian better for witness to Muslims, if combined with a loving heart, than a solid understanding of the nature and character of the triune God – Father, Son and Holy Spirit – as revealed in the Bible.

Appendix A:
Tables of Comparison – Jesus, the Holy Spirit and YHWH

JESUS AND ISA

The Bible	The Quran
Jesus was born in the village of Bethlehem, and Joseph was with Mary at the time. (Luke 2)	Isa was born in an isolated place, and Mary was alone under a date palm. (Q19:20-25)
Jesus was both a Jewish rabbi, and also the Son of God. (Mark 10:51, Matthew 16:16)	Isa was a Muslim prophet. (Q3:75–79)
Jesus preached the good news of the Kingdom of God: he brought no book. (Mark 1:14-15)	Isa received a book of revelation from Allah known as the Injil. (Q5:45–49)

The Bible	The Quran
Jesus died on the cross and was raised to life on the third day after his death. (The Gospels and the Epistles).	Isa did not die on the cross. (Q4:155-59) On judgement day he will bear witness against Christians and Jews for believing in his death. (Q4:155–159)
Jesus will return to judge all humanity. (Matthew 16:27)	Isa will return to destroy Christianity, and all other religions. He will implement the sharia of Muhammad for all. (The Hadith collections, incl. Sahih Muslim)
Jesus' name means 'YHWH is salvation'. (Matthew 1:21)	The name Isa has no meaning in Arabic, and neither can it be fully explained as a borrowing from any other known language.
Jesus is the Messiah (Matthew 16:16), a term which means 'anointed one'. This was a title used of kings. (1 Samuel 16:13, Psalm 89:20,38).	Isa is referred to as the Masih (Q3:40-44) but Islamic scholars cannot agree on what this title means.
Jesus taught his followers to love their enemies. (Matthew 5:43-45)	Isa taught that those who die fighting for Allah will inherit paradise. (Q9:110-114) Allah commands warfare against Christians and Jews until they surrender and pay tribute. (Q9:29)
Jesus is the 'way, the truth and the life': no one can come to God except through him. (John 14:6)	Christians who seek to follow Isa but reject Muhammad and his message will be condemned to hell. (Q98:5)

THE HOLY SPIRIT
AND THE RUH AL-QUDUS

The Bible	The Quran
There is only one Holy Spirit, the life-giving presence of the living God, and this is referred to repeatedly throughout the Bible. The Holy Spirit is not a creature or any kind of angel.	There seem to be three distinct 'spirits' associated with Allah in the Quran. One, the Holy Spirit or Ruh al-Qudus, is the Angel Jibril (or Gabriel: see Q19:15–19; Q2:90–94; Q16:100–104; Ibn Ishaq). Another 'spirit' is a metaphor for the creative word of Allah. (Q4:165–169) There is also a 'spirit' which is the life-giving breath of Allah (Q15:25–29)
There is a great deal of information about the Holy Spirit in the Bible.	When people asked him, Muhammad stated that only a little knowledge has been given about 'the spirit'. (Q17:85–89)

YHWH AND ALLAH

The Bible	The Quran
YHWH is God's name 'forever'. (Exodus 3:13–15)	Allah is God's name. (The Quran)
Evil is not from YHWH, but wilful rebellion against YHWH. YHWH is the author of good, not evil. (Deuteronomy 32:4; Psalm 92:15; 1 John 1:5)	Allah is the author of both good and evil. (Q91:5–9)

The Bible	The Quran
YHWH can make himself present with and in people and places: this is distinct from his omnipresence. (Exodus 33:14–15; Joel 2:27–29)	Allah is everywhere at once, but nowhere in particular: he indwells nothing. (Q2:109; Q4:125)
YHWH is holy, and his followers should be holy too. (Leviticus 19:1–2)	The Holiness of Allah is rarely referred to in the Quran: it appears to be a minor or secondary attribute of Allah. (Q59:20-24)
Human beings are created in God's image and should seek to be like him. (Genesis 1:26–27; Ephesians 5:1-2)	Nothing in creation is like Allah, and people must not seek to be like him. (Q4:50–54) No human attribute may be associated with Allah, and when people use the same words to describe humans and Allah this is merely a figure of speech.
YHWH loves sinners and reaches out to his enemies in love. (Exodus 34:5–7; 1 John 4:19)	Allah will typically hate those who hate him, and love those who obey him, and he wants people to follow him in this. He is however under no obligation to love, and can love or hate whoever he chooses. (Q3:25–29)
YHWH is faithful to his word, which is unchanging, and he does not lie. (Numbers 23:19) Although God can and often does make conditional promises – including covenants – his inherent faithfulness is not dependent upon human faithfulness, but reflects his utter holiness. (Hebrews 6:17–19; Malachi 3:6)	Allah acts as he pleases and is the 'best of schemers' (Q3:54); he can, without impugning his perfection, abrogate something he has said earlier and replace it with a contradictory word. (Q16:100–104) He is not obligated to follow his covenants, nor does he obligate himself to people in any way. (Q17:85–89)

Appendix B:
Conversation Starters for Dialogue with Muslims

This is not about winning arguments or scoring points, but about creating a space for dialogue about deeper issues, which ultimately appeal to the conscience and touch the heart.

The following questions are designed to open up topics for discussion between Christians and Muslims. There are some questions, which Muslims often ask, such as 'How could God have a son?' It is important to have answers to such questions, but Christians also need questions of their own which they can raise with Muslims.

Questions about God

Do we worship the same God?
Why do you believe this is so?

Is Allah good?
Where does evil come from?
Who made Satan evil?
Can sinful people dwell in God's heaven?

Is Allah personal?
Is Allah with you? How do you experience this?
When do you sense his presence?
David said 'Do not cast me from your presence.' (PSALM 51)
What do you think he meant by this?

Is God holy? Why do you say so?
What does this mean for you personally?
Are people meant to be holy too?
Does this make them like God?
How can people become holy?

Is God good? How can you know this?
Should we be good like him? How?
Jesus said that if we forgive those who wrong us,
we will be like God. (Matthew 6:14) Do you agree?

Is Allah loving? Why do you say so?
How can we experience God's love?
Who does Allah love?
Does Allah love you?

Is God faithful?
Can we count on him to be faithful?
Does he always keep his promises?
Would it reflect badly on God if he didn't?
Is it your personal experience that God is faithful to you?

Questions about salvation

Do you believe that the righteous will always be successful? How does this work?
Do you think that people need a saviour? Who is your personal saviour?

Questions about Jesus and the Bible

Do you believe in the Injil? Shall we read Jesus' words together from the Bible?

What does the word Injil mean in Arabic?
Do you know what the word *euangelion* ('gospel') means?

Did Jesus (Isa) die on the cross? Why do you say so?
Christians believe he was crucified and died.
Do you know why they believe this?

Christian pastors often study Hebrew, so they can read the Jewish scriptures in the original language of the Jewish people. Muslims revere the prophets of the Bible, and the Law of Moses, so do Muslims study Greek or Hebrew as part of their training, so they can read the Bible? Why (not)?

Questions about the meaning of names

What does the name *Ibrahim* mean in Arabic?
Do you know where the name Abraham came from?
(GENESIS 17)

What does the name *Ismail* mean in Arabic?
Do you know how the name Ishmael came about and what it means? (GENESIS 16)

What does *Allah* mean?
Does it matter whether this word has a meaning?
Do you know what was revealed to Moses as the name of God? (EXODUS 3)

What does the name *Isa* mean in Arabic?
Do you know where the name *Jesus* comes from, and what it means?

Isa is callled the Masih in the Quran. What does the word *masih* mean in Arabic and how did this apply to Isa?
Would you like to hear what the word *Messiah* means, and why we call Jesus the Messiah?

Bibliography

Al-'Uthaimin, Shaikh Muhammad as-Saleh. *The Muslim's belief*. Translated Maneh Al-Johani. Undated. www.iad.org/PDF/MBE.pdf (accessed Jan 31, 2005).

Al-Tabari. *Jami' al-Bay'dn fi Tafsir al-Qur'an*. Cairo, 1323–1330.

Arberry, Arthur J. *The Koran Interpreted*. Oxford World's Classics. Oxford: Oxford University Press, 1998.

Basil. *On the Holy Spirit. Nicene and Post-Nicene Fathers*, second series. New York: Christian Literature Company, 8:16–17.

Bat Ye'or. *Islam and Dhimmitude: where civilizations collide*. Cranbury: Fairleigh Dickinson University Press/Associated University Presses, 2002.

Bostom, Andrew G. *The legacy of jihad: Islamic Holy War and the fate of non-Muslims*. Amherst, New York: Prometheus Books, 2005.

Democracy is a religion: www.iisna.com/articles/democracy.htm (accessed Oct 10, 2002).

Faris, Nabih Amin (trans. & ed.). *The book of idols, being a translation from the Arabic of the Kitab Al-Asnam by Hisham Ibn-al-Kalbi*. Princeton University Press, 1952.

Gabriel, Mark A. *Islam and the Jews*. Lake Mary, Florida: Charisma House, 2003.

Guillaume, A. *The Life of Muhammad: a translation of Ibn Ishaq's Sirat Rasul Allah*. Karachi & Oxford: Oxford University Press, 1955.

Hopkins, Jasper. *Nicholas of Cusa's De Pace Fidei and Cribratio Alkorani*. 2nd ed. Minneapolis: Arthur J. Banning Press, 1990.

Hughes, T. P. *Dictionary of Islam*. New Delhi: Cosmo, 1885 (2nd reprint 1978).

Ibn Warraq (ed). *What the Koran really says: language, text and commentary*. Amherst: Prometheus Books, 2002.

Keller, Nuh Ha Mim. *Reliance of the Traveller.* The classical manual of Islamic sacred law *'Umdat al-Salik* by Ahmad ibn Nqib al-Misri (d.769/1368) in Arabic with facing English text, commentary, and appendices. Revised ed. Beltsville, Maryland: Amana Publications, 1994.

Khan, Muhammad Muhsin. *The translation of the meanings of the Sahih Al-Bukhari.* 9 vols. Riyadh: Darussalam, 1997.

Madhi, Shaikh Ibrahim. Friday Sermon on Palestinian Authority TV. Memri Special Dispatch Series 370. 2002. http://memri.org/bin/articles.cgi?Page=archives&Area=sd&ID=SP37002

McAuliffe, Jane Dammen. *Encyclopedia of the Qur'an.* Leiden: Brill, 2001–2004.

Newton, P. & M. Rafiqul Haqq. *Allah: is he God?* Columbia: Muslim/Christian Dialogues, 1991.

Nicholas of Cusa — see Hopkins, Jasper.

Sahih Al-Bukhari — see Khan, Muhammad Muhsin.

Sahih Muslim — see Siddiqi, 'Abdul Hamid.

Shapland, C. R. B. *The letters of Saint Athanasius concerning the Holy Spirit.* London: Epworth, 1951.

Shayesteh, Daniel. *A journey from 'gods' to Christ.* Toongabbie: published by Daniel Shayesteh, 2003.

Siddiqi, 'Abdul Hamid. *Sahih Muslim.* Revised ed. 4 vols. New Delhi: Kitab Bhavan, 2000.

Sidiqi, Shamim A. Letter to the editor. *Commentary,* February 2002. www.danielpipes.org/article/117

Sunan Abu-Dawud. Translated Ahmah Hasan. www.usc.edu/dept/MSA/fundamentals/hadithsunnah/abudawud/

Winnett, F. V. 'The Daughters of Allah,' *The Moslem World* 30 (1940), pp.113–130.

Index

Lightning Source UK Ltd.
Milton Keynes UK
13 December 2010

164310UK00009B/125/P

GW00505805

The Work of the Guardian ad Litem

Eva Gregory & Anna Kerr

VENTURE PRESS

Published by
VENTURE PRESS
16 Kent Street
Birmingham
B5 6RD

British Library Cataloguing-in-Publication Data
A catalogue record for this book is available from the
British Library

ISBN 1 86178 024 9   (paperback)

Design, layout and production by
Hucksters Advertising & Publishing Consultants,
Riseden, Tidebrook, Wadhurst, East Sussex TN5 6PA

Cover design by:
Western Arts
194 Goswell Road
London
EC1V 7DT

Printed and bound in Great Britain by
Biddles Limited, Guildford and King's Lynn

Contents

Acknowledgements

The authors would like to acknowledge with gratitude the contribution by Freda Hudson, guardian ad litem, on the chapter *The guardian & other proceedings*; by Susan Howard, assistant panel manager, in compiling the bibliography; and by Kathryn Robinson, solicitor, on preparing Appendix III on Case law relating to the role of the guardian since 1991. This book also draws upon the work done for the earlier *On Behalf of the Child*, published by Venture Press in 1990, written by the present authors together with Freda Hudson and Susan Howard.

NOTE

For the purposes of this book, guardians ad litem will be feminine, solicitors will be masculine, and the child may be of either gender.

The duties and role of the guardian in specified proceedings

This chapter considers the role and defines the primary duties of the guardian in specified proceedings. The proceedings in which a guardian can be appointed are listed, along with a brief discussion of the guiding ideology and philosophy of the Children Act. The chapter concludes with references to the development of national standards and to the aims of developing good practice which is more standardised.

In essence the basic responsibility of the guardian is to safeguard the child's interest in any proceedings brought. To this end the guardian is directed to give first and paramount consideration to the needs of the child, at the same time taking into account their wishes and their feelings and having regard to the child's age and understanding. How the guardian approaches this task has fundamentally changed following the implementation of the 1989 Children Act. Instead of retaining the purely investigative, fact-finding role, the guardian is expected to take on a pro-active stance. This approach then requires the guardian to becoming a mediator, negotiator, resource broker, case manager and monitor.

The Act brought with it numerous other changes. It generally seeks to empower children and to emphasise children's rights to be heard. For instance it allows children (provided they are of an age and understanding), to make their own applications to courts and to refuse to submit to medical or psychiatric examinations. There is an emphasis on greater involvement of parents, who under earlier legislation were frequently marginalised, and the introduction of the concept of the parental responsibility, even for children who are subject to statutory orders.

Another change arising out of the philosophy of the Act is the assumption that there will be reasonable contact between parents, siblings and children who have been removed from home to alternative care. Similarly the Act introduces the concept of partnership between courts, (usually justices clerks and guardians) in order to avoid delays, and ensure that cases are allocated to appropriate courts and cases are efficiently timetabled.

Although the Act has not done away with the adversarial approach to proceedings, it does emphasise the inquisitorial model. Yet the tensions between arriving at a fair and just decision and determining the best interest of the child still exist. Guardians have to be aware of these tensions and must be satisfied that making an order in relation to a child will be better than making no order at all. And before they make their recommendations, they must have scrutinised and considered the details of the plans of the local authority.

1. APPOINTMENT OF A GUARDIAN AND RELEVANT PROCEEDINGS.

At any stage in the proceedings, the court may of its own motion appoint a guardian. Where it refuses to do so, the court has to record this on the appropriate form as defined in the court rules. All the parties to the case would have to be notified of such a decision. When appointing a guardian, the court is expected to consider the appointment of anyone who has previously acted for the same child or children. In practical terms this may not always be possible. The appointment of a guardian continues for the length of time as specified by the court, usually this means until the case is solved judicially. A guardian's appointment can only be terminated by the court, which has to give its reasons in writing. The 1989 Children Act extended the guardian's duties, resulting in being appointed in the following specified proceedings.

- Application for a care or supervision order, Section 31
- Application for a contact order relating to a child in care, Section 34
- Application for a child assessment order, Section 43
- Application for an emergency protection order, Section 44

- Application for a secure accommodation order, Section 25
- Application for an extension of a supervision order, sched.3.p.(6) (3)
- Application for a change of surname or removal from the UK of a child subject to a care order, section 39
- Revocation of a care or supervision order, section 39
- Direction given to a local authority, with the court considering making an interim care or supervision order, section 37

At present (February 1998) guardians cannot act in private law proceedings. There are occasions when guardians are involved in care proceedings for one child in the family whose siblings are involved in private law proceedings. If the unmarried parent then decides to apply for a residence order on these other children, the guardian is not allowed by law to be involved, as these are not specified proceedings. However, in the course of care proceedings courts can make what are known as section 8 orders, such as a residence order, contact order, prohibited steps order or specific issue order. All these orders need to be carefully considered by guardian and solicitor when it comes to deciding on the recommendation.

2. PRIMARY TASKS OF THE GUARDIAN

These can be classified under the following headings. A more detailed description of each subsection will be found in later chapters.

A) INVESTIGATING ALL CIRCUMSTANCES

The guardian is expected to investigate all the circumstances in relation to the child (or children) who is the focus of proceedings. This stage involves numerous preliminary tasks, such as appointing a solicitor and making a case plan in relation to contacting other people and parties. This stage will then be followed by the start of the investigation, which entails information gathering and possibly focussing the investigation on certain specific areas. The latter may be in dispute or require more detailed inquiry. Although guardians are accorded the status of an expert witness they are expected to provide the court with a view on general child care matters. These aspects are dealt with in the next chapter.

B) SAFEGUARDING THE CHILD'S INTERESTS

Guardians will inevitably be faced with making judgements about what is best for children. They need to be sure that their professional judgements are based soundly on well-validated research and professional experience rather than on personal experience. The primary value system operating in current child care planning is the belief that children should be brought up by their own parents. This should take precedence over any other factors. Guardians need to demonstrate to the courts through their evidence and reports, how they have arrived at their particular recommendation and what frame of reference they have used when coming to their conclusions. A fuller account will be found in the chapter on the guardian and the child.

C) ASCERTAINING THE CHILD'S WISHES AND FEELINGS

The guardian will have to make a judgement fairly early on as to the extent to which a child is able to express his feelings and wishes. The child's age, understanding, language, emotional disturbance or disability will all play a part. Guardians need to be realistic as to what can be achieved in the time span of the proceedings and be clear with the child how this is going to be achieved. The relationship with the child is not a therapeutic or social work one, but a means of informing the court of the child's current situation and views. With very young children, it may only be possible to make deductions about the way they respond or relate to others or to their environment. A fuller description will be found in the chapter on the guardian and the child.

D) PREPARING THE REPORT FOR THE COURT AND RECOMMENDATIONS

Guardian reports should be self-contained and stand on their own. They are the culmination of often lengthy investigation, sometimes negotiation, assessments as part of the procedure, the filing of large amounts of evidence and possibly reports from expert witnesses. Essentially guardians must distinguish between facts and opinions with the aim of presenting hard evidence. Guardians may be challenged on assumptions and value judgements. As guardians are appointed to a wide-ranging group of proceedings, the format cannot be identical for each of

these. However, all reports should pay attention to a core
of essential aspects; these include the following:

> - considering and addressing the welfare checklist;
> - the issues surrounding reasonable contact;
> - the wishes and feelings of the child;
> - the options available to the court, and whether making an
>   order is better than not making an order;
> - the recommendation to the court.

This is more fully discussed in the chapter on report writing.

3. THE ISSUE OF INDEPENDENCE

Guardian panels were established in order for an
independent voice to be available to represent children in
proceedings and to assess the evidence arising from this.
Guardians are expected to act as a safeguard for the child
and must at all times not only have an independent
professional view, but show they have personal
independence and are perceived to be independent by
others. Guardians are personally accountable to the court
for the work they carry out. The decisions they arrive at
are autonomous and are not part of a collective decision
making process. They must show credibility and expertise
at the same time. Sometimes guardians may experience
difficulty in being independent because of some event in
their own personal lives. If this should happen, then it
may be in the child's interest that another panel member
takes over the case, provided this is identified at the
beginning of the case. Perceived independence is more
subtle to establish; the way guardians are judged in
relation to this can depend on behaviour, expressed
views, and how guardians substantiate their judgements
with evidence.

4. THE BACKGROUND TO BECOMING A GUARDIAN

Guardians have to be appointed to a panel, managed by a
panel manager, who is responsible for ensuring that there
are sufficient guardians available to carry out the work
produced by the local courts. The Children Act places the
duty of establishing panels of guardians on local
authorities; each local authority can run their own panel,

can contract this service out to a voluntary organisation or can establish panels in a consortium with other local authorities. Guardians go through an appointment procedure and are usually appointed for a period of three years, after which time they can seek re-appointment for further periods of time. Although the rules do not specify specific qualifications, guardians are expected to be qualified social workers of considerable experience, who have worked in a local authority social service department at some time in their career and who have knowledge of work with children and families. At least three quarters of the existing guardian work force in England and Wales of about 850 guardians are self-employed; the remainder are employed either by local authorities or voluntary organisations.

5. THE ESTABLISHMENT OF NATIONAL STANDARDS

Guardians do not have a professional regulatory body as such. Instead there have been moves, mainly by the Department of Health, to create national professional standards. These were initially published at the end of 1996 by the Department of Health. The stated aims of these standards and the criteria by which panels will aim to implement them is chiefly to improve the guardian service. By setting clear expectations about key areas of required practice, by encouraging the delivery of a professionally competent service which is both fair and without discrimination, it is hoped to encourage greater public confidence in the guardian service. The main intention of the national standards is to provide a framework for the development of both the guardian panel and of the professional.

The guardian as investigator and fact finder

This chapter will discuss the guardian's role as investigator; it will spell out the aims and boundaries of the task and clarify its differences from other related functions.

1. THE AIM OF THE INVESTIGATION

The guardian must make an assessment of the child and his/her total situation to present to the court a full picture of the child, the family, the history, the present and future situation. She is not the child's social worker, a legal representative, a psychiatrist or a detective – the role rests somewhere between these positions – a kind of psychological detective – accumulating information and working towards the denouement of the final report.

The **investigation** needs to cover:

- The child's individual history, including physical and educational experience and development;
- The child's own account of his or her life, and hopes for the future;
- The family history, including family relationships and changes in these over time;
- The child's and the family's ethnic, religious, language and cultural experiences and practices;
- The build-up to the case coming to court;
- The child's current situation;
- The child's present and past attachments and experiences of loss and change;
- The significant people and places in the child's past and present life;
- Any professional intervention in the child's life, to include school, social services, health, psychiatric or any other worker involved, and its quality and duration. One must look at what is needed and available for the future;
- The quality and quantity of risk or cause for concern and prognosis for the future.

The **prognosis** needs to offer a well argued and evidenced assessment of the child's present and future needs. This is tricky, relying on information from the past, individual professional experience and information from research to forecast the future. It is hard to make guesses based on incomplete information – particularly when the guardian cannot be sure how well the recommended professional resources will survive. It is tempting to sit on the fence and invite the court to take the decision – but the guardian has a duty to offer a view at the end of the day – to have the final professional word before the matter is turned over to the judgement of the court.

The **prognosis** must consider:

1. The child's present and future needs in relation to:
   - physical and psychological health;
   - safety;
   - physical care.
   - emotional support and nurture;
   - emotional boundaries;
   - education;
   - preparation for work and training in the future;
   - maintenance of kinship links;
   - identity development;
   - maintenance and development of ethnic, religious or cultural ties and practices.

2. The potential for emotional; or physical harm or neglect of the child in the family as compared with the care alternatives.

3. Having identified the areas needing change in the child's carers, their potential for change linked to the likelihood of the provision of the necessary help.

4. The care, treatment and educational alternatives to the family realistically available to the child.

2. THE GUARDIAN'S STANCE

As a social and psychological detective, the guardian rather resembles the detective of crime fiction from the earlier part of the century, Agatha Christie's Hercule Poirot, or Patricia Wentworth's Miss Silver, for instance. Like these all-seeing figures who *"owed no duty to any man except the truth"*, the guardian owes no duty to the local authority or the parents, or any other party, except the best interests of the child.

Essentially forensic, overseeing and fair-minded, the guardian has to tread a careful line between several obvious pitfalls. There is the quasi child therapist, over-identified with the child as victim, who can easily overreach the role and offer the child expectations of rescue and long term relationship which cannot be fulfilled. There is the quasi social work manager, who moves in on the local authority and cannot resist supervising the social worker, competing with the team manager, and doing resource search work the department should be doing for itself. Finally, there is the quasi parent counsellor, whose primary identification is with the parents in their sense of being misunderstood and unsupported and who arouses unreal expectations of being able to make things happen differently or offer a therapeutic alliance.

Which path attracts a guardian depends on the experience and bent of the guardian and the needs of the case. It is much more difficult to hold back from getting too close to parents, if they are at loggerheads with the local authority and are in great need of therapeutic understanding, or to resist taking over the case management if the social worker and manager are at sea and obvious and available resources are being missed. The authors believe that guardians set the scene for their style and stance from the outset of the case.

The guardian is an independent social investigator, preparing a full report for the court on the child's behalf. This has two key ramifications:

● **THE ISSUE OF INDEPENDENCE FROM ALL OTHER PARTIES**
She must be and must be seen to be independent of and separate from the local authority or any other professional or statutory body – other than the court. The child and the family must have the opportunity to relate to and speak to the guardian in a fresh way, free of the history and expectations which may attach to the local authority. She must avoid the temptations we have already discussed.

● THE ISSUE OF ETHNIC DIFFERENCE

The guardian needs to be as vigilant and self-monitoring as possible about the issues of culture, religion, language, ethnicity and colour; more than lip service must be paid to "ethnic awareness". We suggest that whenever a guardian is dealing with a family from a culture, language, colour or religion different from her own she should, as a matter of course, consult with an appropriate source or expert, both at the beginning of the case and at the report preparation stage. Guardians should not take for granted their ability to understand or communicate; they should check out mutual perceptions with the family members. They must also remember, if they are white European, that they cannot ever know what the experience of being foreign in speech or appearance is like, or how it feels to live as a minority black or Asian person in a white majority country, where racist overtones and undertones persist.

In summary, the needs of the child must always be tested against considerations of culture, language, country of origin, religion and colour. Guardians need to be both sensitive and well-informed as well as robust in dealing with this complex and delicate area. Over-simplification of issues of race and culture from a black as well as from a white perspective need to be questioned and examined. Many children guardians meet are from a mixed racial background; respect and attention is required for both sides of their heritage, as well as an awareness of how they will present and be received in general.

3. THE INVESTIGATION

THE FIRST STAGE (FROM APPOINTMENT TO THE FIRST HEARING)

The first task, on first receiving the case, is to make up the file, fill out some type of case front, recording key data about the case, and think about the investigation strategy. The guardian should commit some thoughts to paper, in the form of some kind of case plan; some prefer a detailed plan, some write down a type of brainstorm or thoughts and impressions before highlighting key issues, others prefer to use a checklist. It is worth keeping this early hypothesis/plan/initial set of impressions at the front of the file for reference and re-reference as the case progresses.

Here is an opening procedure before going into action which can be used, adapted or reacted to:

ON FIRST RECEIVING THE REFERRAL

> - Appoint solicitor, notify court of appointment and set up an early discussion. Agree who will pursue which papers.
> - Read and think about the information you have.
> - Open and file your case.
> - Write down your own type of action plan.

HOW TO OBTAIN NECESSARY PAPERS

From the court, the local authority, your solicitor.

WHOM TO CONTACT FIRST

Cases vary in their needs; so do guardians in their preference. Cases starting with an emergency protection order or a secure accommodation order require an early approach to the local authority and appointment to see the child. Some guardians and panels prefer and produce introductory pamphlet, some make their own means of approach. The first contact can be significant and the flavour for what follows. It is a good idea, in our view, to see all the most significant people fairly close together within the first week or so.

These are likely to be the social worker, the child, the parents and other carers. Each will make a particular impact on ones sensibilities and judgement; it is better to move on to the next fairly quickly in early stages, keeping the mind and feelings as open as possible. Aim to feel and project a friendly, courteous, enquiring, neutral attitude. This works both ways: parents, social workers and children will be struck by and will remember your manner and approach as they first encounter you.

LIST THOSE WHO NEED SEEING IN THE FIRST FEW WEEKS, WHERE, AND WITH WHOM

This includes considering with the solicitor when he should see the child. (This is discussed more fully in the chapter: *The guardian and the legal system*).

SUMMARISE INFORMATION AND PRELIMINARY VIEW REQUIRED FOR FIRST HEARING

This may be imminent and the guardian must consider whether a preliminary view is to be offered, or whether she has to let the court and parties know that it is too early for this. Consider whether you can let the court know the child's wishes at this stage, either directly if he or she is old and confident enough to communicate them, or indirectly, via an early assessment. This may be possible, and the guardian needs to seek an adjournment to give time to come to a preliminary view.

Case example

A guardian was appointed two days before a first hearing to consider the local authority's application for an interim care order for eight weeks to allow them to asses the special needs of 6-year-old Tony with delayed language and autistic features, His parents were embattled and unable to co-operate or communicate and the plan was to place Tony in a foster home twenty miles distant. The guardian could not form a view without having seen the child or met any of the parties before the hearing, and did not think it right, from the papers, to adopt a neutral position and allow the court to decide. A week's adjournment was agreed by all parties, the child remained at home, the local authority looked for a closer foster home and the guardian had time to make her basic enquiries.

NOTE DOWN FIRST IMPRESSIONS.

You could try writing down a few key phrases, such as,

"Colourful, chaotic situation, social worker seems lost, as does child. Case feels tricky. Watch out."

THE MIDDLE STAGE. (FROM FIRST HEARING TO REPORT PREPARATION).

This is the very important part of the process – in some ways the most crucial and the least exciting. You can get used to the case, the first thrill dies down and you get stuck in the mire of heavy case files, conflicting personalities and demands, and the volume of work which must be done thoroughly.

The outline of the case having been set at the first hearing (through probably not the full legal timetable and agenda), the guardian must get down to careful planning (preferably in consultation with the solicitor) about:

> A. who to see;
> B. who to consult;
> C. case management issues;
> D. what to read;
> E. order of operation;
> F. possible timetable;
> G. legal issues (e.g. level of jurisdiction);
> H. any special or unusual considerations or issues (see B).

A & B. WHO TO SEE AND CONSULT

The child, the parent/s and the social worker must be seen. The child must be seen on his or her own and with parents. These are minimum requirements. Key family members, significant friends or local figures, teachers, other professionals should be seriously considered.

The child. This is considered in the chapter on the guardian and the child.

The parents. The guardian must see them at least once in their own home. Issues of safety need remembering here; guardians can take a colleague or arrange for the parents' solicitor to be present, if need be. Other interviews can take place in the solicitor's or other appropriate office. The guardian is primarily aiming to gain information and form a view, rather than to set up a therapeutic alliance. However, one needs to be courteous and reasonably sympathetic in approach. The main snare is: *"You really seem to understand, not like that block of stone of a social worker who only wants to catch me out and take Stacey away. You're not like that, you care".* Very seductive, but beware – who knows what your view will be about to Stacey at the end of the day.

Other people in the child's life, personal and professional. Adopt the same stance, and aim to gain information to build up your picture of the child's life and needs. Always bear in mind what anyone might be able to offer to the child in the future; investigation is both about what has gone wrong already and what may be on offer for the future. You might consider seeing someone who seems significant for the future together with the child to test this out, or going back to the child and talking to him/her about that person.

The guardian needs constantly to check and re-check in their mind which professionals should be interviewed: the local authority social worker, the child's class teacher, any other professional involved in the case. This might be a health visitor, a GP or a specialist, like a child psychiatrist or worker with specialist expertise. It is always worth considering whether to interview the social worker's manager and/or the head teacher. Both may have valuable information about the child, can give an overall picture of their agency's strengths and weaknesses and also have management authority. In particular, the guardian should always introduce herself to the social worker's manager, (in case of future need).

If a case runs and runs, the guardian will probably have to go back for a second meeting with parties and other professionals, to see how they are faring over time and perhaps to test out information gained since they were first interviewed.

C. CASE MANAGEMENT ISSUES

Here, the balance must be held between taking over from the social worker and letting the case drift along during the judicial process. The guardian has a duty to oversee what is happening for the child and how the case is progressing through the court, but must avoid directing operations in place of the local authority. Occasionally, the line is crossed in the child's interests but this will be the exception.

Case example

A guardian was appointed for a contact application by a sibling of the birth mother to a 5-year old boy in care, Leon, who was about to be placed for adoption with a couple who were opposed to any form of contact with the birth family. On first reading of the papers, it seemed to the guardian that such contact would benefit Leon who used to know his aunt and uncle well The guardian tried to persuade the social worker to delay placement: when this was refused, she had to take the case back to court for a direction to the local authority not to place the child until the guardian had investigated the circumstances. Subsequent inquiry eventually led to Leon being placed to live with his aunt and uncle. This was an exceptional circumstance, but one in which action was merited.

The key issue for every case, by definition, is going to be the viability of the child living at home with his or her family. From the beginning of proceedings, the guardian must be thinking about how the assessment of this can best be made: by observing contact, by using an expert resource, such as a child psychiatrist or psychologist, or a specialist day centre, or whether the family is suitable for residential assessment. The latter will be the only option in some cases, and it is important to know the residential facilities well; there is variation in quality and stance, and the match between a family and a resource needs consideration. The authors are wary of residential assessment centres where staff are enthusiastic but unsophisticated and not well supported professionally, and at the other end of the spectrum, we are aware of certain disorganised and emotionally chaotic families who are bound to fail in high-powered centres with a great emphasis on fitting into their systems.

The local authority should keep the guardian informed of events during the court process; the guardian has a responsibility to make sure this happens and in turn to keep the child's solicitor updated.

D. WHAT TO READ

The guardian must read all local authority files and all documents before the court. Additionally she should check if there are other crucial papers to be read, for example, the records of any other agency, case files with another local authority previously involved, private letters or papers relevant to the child.

The importance and length of time required for this activity should never be underestimated. People's histories, once recorded, become congealed and sealed over time and must always be taken with a pinch of salt. There is the apocryphal but plausible story of the client seen waiting by the roadside, who, by a series of rumours passed from person to person, became labelled as a working prostitute. Something is not true because it is written down in a social work file. It is useful to have a technique for recording and highlighting information for easy future reference.

E, F & G ORDER OF OPERATION, TIMETABLE AND LEGAL ISSUES
The order of operation is flexible and needs to be adjusted
to the needs of the case. The timetable and other legal
issues are discussed more fully in the chapter on the
guardian and the legal system.

H ANY SPECIAL OR UNUSUAL CONSIDERATIONS
This includes the child's ethnicity, religion and language,
any considerations of disability, any special issues of his or
her ordinal position (for example, twinship, or
relationship to other siblings).

THE FINAL STAGE OF THE INVESTIGATION
(Up to closure of the case)

At this point, the guardian should check carefully whether
she has all the information necessary to write the report
and offer the court a recommendation. This can be gone
over with the solicitor and checked against the original
and subsequent case plans. It may be that the guardian
will have to go back to the case files, or perhaps interview
someone hitherto overlooked, even at this late stage. It is
better to be over zealous than under prepared.

The guardian as case manager

This chapter will consider the guardian's pivotal role in specified child care proceedings, the deployment of strategies in order to move the case along and secure for the child what is in his best interest and bring about an outcome.

Guardians need to be aware that they play a pivotal role in any specified proceedings concerning children. They are seen as being the driving force in the process and having considerable influence on the way a case progresses through the courts. Increasingly they are seen as managing the case through the proceedings. The Department of Health has encouraged this role of case manager, so that a sense of purpose and direction is achieved. Guardians are able to intervene at intervals (along with other parties) in order to ensure that a change of direction is effected. However, guardians are not responsible for the whole case; they have to be clear about their own role and that of others.

1. GENERAL ROLE

Guardians need to recognise that they are expected to take on a pro-active role throughout the proceedings, to be aware what is happening and to be prepared to advise the courts accordingly. Such a stance will entail a number of activities; some, the guardian will have to initiate on her own, others will have to be done in conjunction with the child's solicitor. The activities are seen to include the following:

- consider whether the case is heard at the appropriate court level;
- maintain a time table as to their own case plan;
- keep an eye on whether the directions ordered by the court are being complied within the timetable;
- review the assessments being carried out and the conclusions drawn from these;
- whether any expert evidence is needed;
- keep in touch with the court either through the clerk but more usefully through the child's solicitor;
- maintain contact with the local authority and other parties, either directly or through their legal representatives.

Throughout this process, the guardian must remain open minded, flexible and not precipitately jump to conclusions. Yet by taking on this pro-active role the guardian can help to avoid unnecessary delay and hopefully retain her focus.

2. PLANNING AND REVIEWING

Following the initial decision to start on the investigation, as described in the previous chapter, guardians need to continually re-appraise what tasks have been achieved so far and what others need to be done. Any guardian assessment will require planning from the outset to be followed by continuous review. It could be that after having made a start on seeing certain people such as relatives of the child, it becomes clear that there are others who should be interviewed. This could be to provide more relevant information or possibly they could play a greater part in the child's life. Having started on this approach of planning and reviewing, it is important that this pattern is maintained throughout the investigation of the case. The guardian must remain creative and continuously think of various options regarding the child's future.

Case example

In a care case concerning Richard, John and Daniel, where after fifteen months of proceedings, in which a rehabilitation programme had been tried, it became clear that the parents' had insufficient capacity to adequately care for these little boys. The most likely outcome appeared a care order with the likelihood of adoption. Just prior to the final hearing, an aunt and uncle put themselves forward as possible future carers. The initial investigation by the guardian suggested that this was an alternative proposal which merited further exploration and assessment. In spite of delays which this would entail, the case was adjourned for four months in order for the relatives to be assessed. This proved positive, and the children went to live with their relatives on a residence order.

---

3. ADVISING THE COURT ON SIGNIFICANT OTHERS AND PARTY STATUS

The guardian is expected to advise the court whether there are other people significant to the child, who should be made party to the proceedings, having first ascertained with the relevant party, their willingness to be involved in this way. This could be an unmarried father or grandparents. They may not necessarily become carers in due course, but may well be able to play an active role in relation to the past or the future of the child. They may have information which needs to be put into a statement and which can then be tested in court through evidence, rather than as information given to the guardian in the course of her inquiries. Information collected in this way is useful, but in some instances the court needs to learn at first hand certain views. No one can attend a hearing or be able to put such views, unless they are either an expert and have filed a report or are parties to the proceedings and have filed a statement.

The guardian's advice can include other options such as alternative orders. These could provide a different solution for the child.

Case example

Claudette and Marcia were two young girls of mixed race background who lived with their single mother. The latter managed to care for her children when she was well, but when her mental health deteriorated, her parenting similarly suffered. The children's grandmother had previously played an active role, and maintained contact. However, because of her own commitments, she was unable to take on their care, though she was able to provide support to the family. It seemed that in the children's' interest, it would be prudent to make her a party. She had to be willing and also be prepared to pay lawyers out of her own financial resources, unless she was eligible for legal aid. This is not automatic in such instances, and can only be awarded on merit and means testing.

---

4. TRANSFER OF CASES FROM ONE LEVEL OF COURT TO ANOTHER

The guardian should be prepared to advise the court whether a case should be transferred from one court to a higher court. This can take place at the first directions hearing, when it may already have become clear that the case will either take several days to resolve in a hearing, or where the proceedings are exceptionally complex, grave or important. The guardian needs to be aware whether there are any other simultaneous proceedings pending or taking place in other courts and which relate to this family. Usually consolidation with the current proceedings is the most appropriate solution. All the above proposals should be done in conjunction with the child's solicitor, and having taken soundings from all the other parties.

When making proposals for transfer of cases, the guardian needs to acquire expertise and knowledge as to the likely way the proceedings will develop, to evaluate the time it is likely to take to resolve the issues and how long the final hearing is likely to take. The guardian needs to take into account whether a transfer will create undue delay for the child.

5. TIMETABLING OF PROCEEDINGS

The guardian is expected to take an active role in the time tabling of the proceedings. This may be appropriate at the first directions hearing, or more often, time tabling becomes more productive when there has been some investigation of the matter. This can provide information indicating where the case is going, how long an assessment is going to take place, whether experts are involved and what statements will be required from the various parties. The best way of setting a time table is to obtain dates for the final hearing, when the whole case will be heard and then work backwards, with the guardian's report being the last to be filed with the court. Although the rules stipulate that this should be within seven days of the hearing, it is fairer to the parties if more time is allowed. Courts often plumb for ten to fourteen days. Other statements and reports can then be fitted into the time allowed between the last piece of investigation or assessment and the final hearing. Guardians should remember the domino effect of late statements and that unless they and their solicitors keep a vigilant eye, drift and loss of impetus can set in.

6. THE USE OF EXPERTS

The guardian should take an active role in the use of experts on behalf of the child. The use of experts can be proposed by any party in the proceedings. This could be in order to provide further advice to the court or to question other parties' proposals on the use of experts. As all experts require leave of the court to see the relevant statements and documents, this is an area which should be firmly controlled, in order to avoid a proliferation of experts. The guardian has a powerful voice as to whether experts should be allowed to make assessments of the child in the first instance.

Where it is considered useful that an assessment by an expert will contribute to the proceedings, theexpert will need a letter of instruction. Letters of agreed instructions should be available to all the parties in the proceedings, so that it is clear what the expert is expected to report in.

Case example

Sharif, who was a small baby at the time, was found to have subdural haematoma when his head was X-rayed, the first opinion on the scan suggested that there must have been two injuries at different times probably arising out of shaking the baby. In view of the parents denial that any shaking had taken place, it was important that a further expert opinion was sought on possible cause and difference in timing of the injuries. With the agreement of all parties concerned the guardian was given leave to obtain another opinion.

The guardian and solicitor should be on guard against the inappropriate use of experts. Sometimes psychiatric assessments are requested when the assessment should be carried out by the local authority itself or delegated to others able to make social assessments. On the other hand guardians should be careful not to exceed their own expertise and claim expert knowledge which goes beyond that of their professional expertise as trained social workers. If guardians have other qualifications or specialised knowledge this can be used and needs to be stated in the guardian's report. Guardians should keep a watching brief as to who will be appointed as an expert and their credentials to this role.

Guardians should be prepared to meet with the experts, if there is disagreement in order to establish agreed and disagreed opinions and the reasons for the disparity. Alternatively the guardian can with the help of the solicitor encourage the experts to clarify those issues which remain in dispute between themselves. This could entail a further statement from one or more expert giving reasons for the differing opinion. The court would then have before it issues which remain at variance and those with which the experts agree. At all times guardians should evaluate the expert opinion provided, how much weight to attach to it and what contribution the expert view can make towards the proceedings in order to provide the best outcome for the case.

7. THE USE OF ASSESSMENT FACILITIES

Other approaches can include the use of residential or day facilities which are geared to making family assessments, as well as providing an independent view of parental capacity to parent and of the family dynamics and relationships. Many such establishments are run by voluntary organisations. Some will make an assessment in a matter of weeks, others take several months. Guardians need to be clear what a particular case requires. Referrals should be put in writing with clear requests as to what is required and what the issues are. Any referral to such an establishment will need the agreement of all the parties and the court; leave will need to be obtained for the children to be interviewed, observed and assessed and for court documents to be seen.

8. NEGOTIATING, MEDIATING AND INFLUENCING

The guardian should be prepared throughout the case, to mediate, negotiate and influence the proceedings. This involves maintaining contact with the various parties. These tasks can occur at any time throughout the proceedings. They could include looking at the contact arrangements between parent(s) and children, and whether these should be changed during the course of the proceedings. Continuous appraisal of the situation relating to the children will involve discussions with local authority staff. The guardian can be instrumental in arranging meetings or suggest that the local authority arranges a meeting in order to discuss assessments or rehabilitation, what resources to use etc.. Increasingly it is the guardian's role, to help manage the proceedings in such a way, that issues become less adversarial and more focused. By questioning initial stances and interim plans if these do not seem to be consistent with the child's welfare, by making alternative suggestions, or using alternate resources, a closer rapprochement can often be reached.

Case example

Mary's case came before the courts mainly because of the dysfunctional home environment and the chaotic life style of parents who had difficulty in exerting their authority, yet who showed considerable attachment to their daughter. And she in turn had a bond with them. The crucial problem was Mary's lack of schooling as she had not attended for the last three years, so that by the age of twelve she had missed a great deal of education. The main reason was her phobic symptoms about school and her anxiety leaving home. The local authority's plans were for foster care with attendance at a local special school. The involvement of an independent psychologist, and numerous discussions with the local authority by the guardian persuaded them to rethink their plans. This eventually resulted in Mary going to a weekly boarding school geared to her particular needs. It also meant that the attachment she had to her parents was not broken and that the proposed plans became equally acceptable to them.

---

9. WORKING RELATIONSHIPS WITH THE LOCAL AUTHORITY DURING THE PROCEEDINGS

The guardian should maintain an overview of the progress of the case, by retaining close contact with local authority staff. Guardians are expected to appraise the work of the local authority; this implies that appraisal should not only be negative, but should include a recognition of any positive features and the effort made in a particular situation.

It is important that as soon as contact is made with the local authority staff, the guardian checks out with the social worker their knowledge and expectation of the role of the guardian, and where necessary the guardian's role is clarified.

A pattern should develop in which there is an exchange of relevant information; this may entail the guardian acquiring a vigilant and questioning approach. This will then ensure that changes in situations are notified to the guardian. Similarly, the guardian may become aware of changes in the wishes if the child, and new information becomes available about other parties. Guardians can only make judgements and be influential in cases, if they are aware of developments. This can involve the attendance at meetings, if appropriate, or the arrangement of meetings involving social service personnel, lawyers etc. specific to a particular topic. The initiative for such events can come from the guardian as well as local authority staff.

The extent to which sharing and contact between guardian and local authority staff takes place depends to some extent on the complexity of the case. In situations where matters are fairly straightforward, such as the taking of care proceedings because the baby has been abandoned by its mother, and there are few parties and few contentious issues, the dialogue with the local authority may be more limited. This may be in contrast to proceedings where there are structured plans for rehabilitation, where there are other complex issues and numerous parties, involving considerable dialogue.

10. MONITOR AND DELAY

The guardian should be prepared to monitor delay. It is generally accepted that not all delay is disadvantageous to the child; in some instances it can have a positive application and will be useful to the child. If delay has occurred, then it is important to establish its cause. The reasons for this varies, and will include late reporting by the experts, late filing of statements, overcrowded court agendas and unfulfilled plans. The guardian is in a crucial position to assess if work undertaken by a party to the proceedings has not been carried out satisfactorily within the time scale agreed. Remedies for this can vary from getting the child's solicitor to make inquiries, to seeking a directions hearing and adjudication by the courts. The guardian may argue for delaying the final hearing in cases where an assessment or a rehabilitation plan has to be completed before final decisions can be made. In others, where there are uncertainties in the final care plan, such as whether the local authority will pay a residence allowance, the guardian may think it appropriate to delay making a final recommendation until the disputed areas are resolved.

Case example

It was agreed that following the breakdown of rehabilitation plans, it was not possible for Barbara to care for her four children. They had been placed with a foster family on a short-term basis with a view to assessing the feasibility of rehabilitation. Because of the bonding, and the attachment of the children to their mother and their age it was agreed that plans should be made for long term fostering. The current fostercarers had indicated that they would be prepared to be considered for this role on certain conditions. When it came to the final hearing, the local authority had not established whether they were prepared to take on a long term commitment, and made different proposals such as splitting the children up and seeking adoption for two of them. The guardian argued that these new plans were not in the best interests of the children; that although there should be a care order eventually, the final hearing should be adjourned until the assessment had been completed with a view to long- term care. Additionally, the care plans needed to be reconsidered. Although this introduced delay in the way the matter would be disposed of, the delay was positive and constructive and resulted in an outcome which was best for these children.

The guardian and the child

This chapter will look at the guardian's direct contact with the child and its purpose. The aims of the assessment of the child are discussed in the chapter on the guardian as investigator and fact finder.
A word of warning: the authors consider the commonly used term "working with children" to be a misnomer for the guardian's activity. Guardians, we believe, should not "work with" children, they are not offering a therapeutic relationship; rather they need to create rapport in order to:

- explain and interpret the judicial process to the child;
- discover the child's wishes and feelings and report them to the court;
- make an appraisal of the child's needs;
- monitor the impact of the court process on the child throughout the proceedings.

Each case is about and for the child: this must be held in the forefront of the guardian's mind throughout the process. Guardians as litem are appointed essentially to stand for the child's interests and conscious and unconscious hopes and fears, and to keep a focus in place through the conflicts and complexities of the bureaucratic and judicial process. Although guardians are appointed by courts and funded by local authorities, they struggle to remain autonomous and independent from the state : to stand for the smallest and least powerful figure caught between public and parental forces.

1. STARTING OFF

On appointment to the case, the guardian needs to think where to meet the child. Usually it is best to start off where they are based, at home or in care, and to involve the adults they know. With a child of a suitable age and understanding, a guardian can write in advance and send an appropriate leaflet.

It helps the child to have something physical to hold onto; to see and to keep – a leaflet, explanatory letter, photo or card. It enhances the reality of the guardian and gives a message that the child matters and is being treated seriously.

2. INTRODUCTORY SESSION

The guardian needs to introduce herself properly right at the beginning and repeat this definition of the role, and its limitations, at intervals throughout her acquaintance with the child. It is critical for guardians to define their professional identity clearly for the child and to remember that they are trying to create a rapport within which to get to know and represent the child's position. Some aspects of the following messages need to be conveyed to the child, usually over a series of interviews, depending on age and understanding:

"I am from the family court and I am your guardian ad litem. This means that I work for you and tell the court about you. All children in the family courts have guardians, you may know other children in this children's/foster home who have guardians. I am a guardian to other children, some the same age as you. This is my card for you to keep. This is my name and how you can reach me."

"I will be your guardian all the time the court is thinking about you, when the court is over, we will say goodbye. The court has to decide what is best for you. They take time to do this and you will live at... while they do that."

"I have to write a report for the court about you. I have to tell the court your age – if you are a boy or a girl – what you are like (to cover religion, ethnicity, language) – about your family and your school – about your life – what you need and what you want. I'm not your social worker or your solicitor or foster carers. I don't have to agree with others – not even your parents."

The guardian must remember to keep checking out the child's understanding, particularly that they grasp the difference from their social worker and solicitor.

Guardians should consider the question of timescale with the child and let them know they will keep in touch throughout the court process. They might consider doing a sketch of the court layout and/or a diagram for the child placed in the middle and lines of communication going out to relevant people in their life and the court process.

Case example

This illustrates a trap a guardian fell into in her attempt to establish a friendly rapport with a child. The guardian visited 8-year-old Ivy in her foster home two days after she had been taken there via an Emergency Protection Order in the middle of the night. The child wanted to go back to her mentally ill mother and perceived the social worker as persecutory to her and her Mum. The guardian introduced herself as *"someone different from the social worker who will advise the court... and wants to hear what your feelings and wishes are"*. Ivy fell eagerly on this offer (which seemed to her like a promise), hoping for support of a reunion with her mother, about whom she was very worried. The guardian failed to stress that she could not necessarily deliver the child's wish. This led to disappointment and lack of trust for the remainder of the court process.

The guardian should consider taking a photograph of the child at some point in the proceedings. This may be useful to show or give to a parent to relative who is distant from the child, and it adds to the court's feeling for the child if a photograph can be displayed. It also (usually) seems to make a positive experience for the child to be photographed – making him or her feel worthwhile and valued by the guardian. It may not be appropriate in all cases, particularly when the child is suspicious and wary of authority.

3. COMMUNICATION TECHNIQUES

There are many techniques guardians use to interview and communicate with children, depending on the child's age, emotional state, disability, the venue, who else is present and the guardian's own experience and preference. The guardian must remember the child's language ability and cultural background

The following are some ideas for communicating

with/gaining understanding of child. The main general point is that one needs to be personally comfortable with any tool or technique used. They can be tried out in advance on a child known socially. Children sense quickly if an adult is ill at ease or play-acting, and it increases anxiety on both sides. Guardians can think whether they prefer to introduce an item specially or have it available and see what the child chooses to use.

- Pens and paper.
- "We'll draw an island together and put anything we like on it" (and many other similar ideas individuals may create).
- BAAF (British Agency for Adoption and Fostering) drawing sheets.
- Draw your family. Talk about them.
- Draw family home, foster home etc. (To get an idea of pattern of life, sleeping & eating arrangements, animals etc.)
- Ladder of houses lived in (to get an idea of history, moves disruptions, separation events).
- Dolls or small animals, which lend themselves to become family members.
- Happy Families card game.
- Toy telephones. Some children talk with less anxiety to a professional or to imaginary others through the phone, or to a toy or doll.
- Similarly, some children like to use glove puppets as ways of communicating.
- Games to use to relax, e.g. dominoes, snakes and ladders, cards.
- Computers.

Many of these kind of tools and techniques can also be used in the company of others – other children in the household, parents or parental figures – both to relax and bring some ease into the session and as a means of understanding the child's interaction with others. Guardians must not assume that children from different backgrounds share their assumptions about the meaning of play and language

It is unwise to show a drawing to the court accompanied by an interpretation; most guardians are not qualified to do this. However, a drawing can be appended to give the court a sense of the child.

Children vary so enormously in social and emotional

development that one has to be sensitive and flexible. It cannot be assumed that a 15-year-old will be contemptuous of play material, or that a small child will jump on soft toys with delight. The professional confidence the guardian brings to the meeting is critical; this will be anxiety-reducing and will provide a safe enough feeling for the child and guardian to experiment together. Many guardians find it works best to take a selection of materials and items with them, show them to the child or young person in an easy manner and see what happens. If things are sticky and fraught, one can start doodling oneself, leaving pens lying around, or playing with plasticine or laying out small dolls in groups.

Guardians are not creating a psychotherapeutic relationship, yet can adapt some child psychotherapy methodology, particularly the use of non-directive, open play. Self awareness will help a guardian know if she has an inclination towards over-identification with the child and a "child rescue" over-orientation. Some guardians have this bent, and they need to watch themselves carefully and keep in role towards the child or change jobs and take up direct therapeutic work with children.

Case example

This illustrates the way 7-year-old Winston used a toy to communicate his feelings, an episode which was described in the guardian's report, to great effect. Winston and his younger brother, Glenroy, were in long term foster care, and wanted to go home or see more of their mother. They were mistrustful of the social worker and the guardian, and Winston rarely spoke to carers or official visitors. By contrast, he was lively and spontaneous at school and on contact visits. The guardian (who knew the child quite well at this time and had seen him at home) laid out toys and drawing materials and tried to engage him in conversation on a visit to the foster home. Winston was withdrawn and sullen until the end of the visit, when he picked up a small plastic figure of an elf made of linking plastic parts. He separated the torso and head from the lower body at the waist, and handed the top half to the guardian. *"Give this to Mummy"*, he said, *"And I'll keep this bit"*, and he put the bottom part into his pocket.

---

4. OLDER CHILDREN

While some older children do respond to play and activity, some may be disdainful, withdrawn, entirely silent, fearful, or apparently deeply hostile. The more the guardian can be, and appear to be, at ease herself, the more it becomes possible that the young person will be able to settle and talk.

However, total silence is a communication in itself, which can be commented on, noted and shared with the court. It is worth saying to the mute young person, *"I note that you're not saying anything to me. I wonder why that is." "If you don't want to say anything at all, that is your right, and I will let the court know that is how you feel"*.

If the child is old enough to give his or her own instructions, the guardian needs to take particular care in explaining the difference between the guardian and the solicitor's role. This is discussed more fully in Chapter 6. In our experience, this can be one of the most confusing things for the child to understand, and it can be seen to devalue the guardian in the child's eyes.

Case example

14-year-old Lois was out of her parents' control, refusing to go to school and running away from home into dangerous situations. For nine months, the local authority responded to the parents' pleas for help by accommodating her in a local children's homes, from which she immediately ran away whereupon the parents welcomed her back. Finally she overdosed fairly seriously and the local authority took an emergency protection order and placed her in a small unit in the depths of the countryside with one-to-one staff supervision. The parents felt ambivalent, but finally agreed unhappily to an 8-week interim care order at the first hearing. The guardian supported the order and Lois showed her contempt for the guardian by total silence. Her solicitor contested the order on her behalf, unsuccessfully and Lois's only words to the guardian were, *"I thought you were for me – why couldn't you agree with me?"*

At the next hearing, a further interim was sought; again, Lois was the only one in disagreement. By this time, the plan was for a phased return home with educational and therapeutic support, the local authority working in conjunction with the parents to this end. At this hearing, the guardian again supported the order, and the solicitor had to explain to Lois that she could not contest it again, but could only tell the court she was not opposing the mother. Lois felt dissatisfied with both guardian and solicitor, and told them they were the same as everybody else.

---

5. THE DIFFERENCE BETWEEN THE INDIRECT AND THE DIRECT APPROACH

We believe that the guardian, as well as trying to win the child's confidence, perhaps in some of the ways suggested above, does need to speak directly to the child's mind and conscious understanding. The child needs to know, in some form of words, that the guardian has to tell the court what their wishes and feelings are and to be given an opportunity to put them in their own words.

When the guardian is about to prepare the report, the child may be invited to write a letter to the court, the text to be included in the report. They can write it this themselves or to dictate it to the guardian. Many children do respond to this offer; they seem to feel that the process is serious and that their views matter.

Direct questions can be phrased in varying ways; a child might be asked: *"Is there anything about your Mum/Dad/home you'd like to be different before you go home?"* (perhaps a less disloyal idea). It is crucial to mention in the report whether the child has been asked directly about the key issues in his/her life – comment on why not.

6. ESCORTING THE CHILD THROUGH THE COURT PROCESS

The following points must be kept in mind:

- Keep in loose but reliable touch with the child – the whole process is often very long drawn out. In our opinion, this does not mean visiting the child regularly for the sake of it, or as an overinvolved therapeutic enterprise. One can keep in touch by telephoning the carer, and asking to be remembered to the child, by the occasional note. Visits, especially to the child, should only be made for a good purpose;
- Let the child know if there are any major changes in the judicial process, for example, if new parties have come on the scene who affect the alternatives, or if the final hearing date has been adjourned;
- Think about where, how and when children should meet their solicitor. This should be decided jointly with the solicitor, who will want to see all children of the age of understanding (arguable, but probably from at least 9 years old). However, the guardian needs to have his or her own view about this; ▶

- Similarly, if other experts or outsiders for whom the guardian is responsible are to be brought in, think about how to prepare the child and where/how the meeting should take place;
- Check out the child's understanding of the process and the guardian's role from time to time;
- Think about the child's involvement in the final hearing. Children are becoming less seen in court, particularly in county or high courts. Nevertheless, it is a matter the guardian should consider. One might at least show a child an empty court room to help them visualise where the deliberations about them will be taking place;
- Take the responsibility for the child knowing and understanding as well as possible the outcome of the case. This may be via another person, parent or professional, or by letter, or in person from the guardian or solicitor;
- Take care with leave taking from the child, however and wherever this happens. It should not be unexpected, and should be clearly understood to be final. Some guardians give children a leavetaking card, booklet or sheet of paper, laying out the court's decision and noting names, roles and responsibilities for the child in future.

In conclusion, the following are obligatory (except with very good reason, which should be explained to the court):

- All children must be seen on their own, at least once;
- Siblings should be seen together, as well as individually;
- Children must be seen with their parent/s or significant carer or relative under consideration (for example, where a grandparents is being assessed);
- Refer to Welfare Checklist in the report and in your thinking about the child;
- In adoption, (depending on age) children must be asked directly if they understand meaning of the Order and if it is what they want.

The duties and role of the guardian in adoption

This chapter considers briefly the role of the guardian in adoption. It also describes the task of the reporting officer. Although there were indications in 1995 and 1996 that new legislation would be proposed in order to make adoption legislation more consistent with the Children Act, this is now in abeyance. This chapter touches briefly on inter-country adoption, on issues aroused by trans-racial adoption and the crucial question of children retaining contact with birth parents. Once upon a time adoption was a means of providing a service to childless couples by arranging for the adoption of illegitimate babies. For the last twenty five years adoption has increasingly become a service to children within the spectrum for finding permanent provision of them. The statistics show that adoption has declined from its heyday. Far fewer younger children are adopted, and those that are, tend to have special needs or specific problems. The majority of children who are adopted are over the age of five. Adoption means the legal transfer of a child from one family to another family.

1. THE GUARDIAN'S TASK

There are two main sets of circumstances in which a guardian is appointed in adoption proceedings:

- in circumstances where the birth parent or parents are unwilling to give their consent to the adoption;
- in situations where the court considers that there are special features requiring investigation, even if the birth parent is willing. This would apply where there is an inter-country adoption, or one parent has a mental health problem and may not understand the implications, or an adoption application has been made by relatives, or fostercarers and does not have the support of the local authority as adoption agency, or where both parents are dead or missing.

The guardian's brief is more limited in adoption than in care proceedings. By the time the guardian arrives on the scene, having been appointed by the court, the child(ren) are in their potential adoptive home, the placement has been approved and the agency plan could be to write the parent(s) out of the script. Much of the assessment and preparation has been carried out by the adoption agency. The guardian has several tasks: firstly, to decide whether the parents are withholding their consent unreasonably and whether it is in the child's interest for this consent to be dispensed with so that the adoption can go ahead; secondly to consider the issue of direct and indirect contact with birth parents and siblings post-adoption; thirdly whether an adoption order is the right order in these circumstances; and lastly whether the adoption placement is in the child's best interest. It is rare for guardians to remove a child already settled but it is theoretically possible.

Guardians may be appointed to adoption cases by magistrates courts, county courts or the High Court. In adoption hearings, the child cannot be made a party in the first two levels of jurisdiction. Children are always parties to the proceedings in the High Court; this means that the guardian has to appoint a solicitor. In complex circumstances in the county court, the guardian may request the court to be made a party so that the guardian can be legally represented. In those situations, the guardian needs to clarify who will be responsible for their costs.

2. APPROACHING THE TASK

The legislation which regulates the adoption process and provides for the appointment of guardians or reporting officers is to be found among a number of documents and court rules. (see bibliography at end of book). Following appointment, the court will send the guardian the adopters' application, the child's birth certificate, the marriage certificate of the adopters and the schedule 2 report. The latter is a comprehensive report written by the adoption agency in whose area the child lives. Guardians should not start their investigations until they have received the latter document. The adoption agency is supposed to lodge this with the court, six weeks after the adopters' application has been made. In practice there are often delays and guardians may have to badger the court or the agency to produce this report. Guardians are expected to scrutinise the schedule 2 report, and may have to send it back if there are gaps or inaccurate information.

Adopters can be single or married applicants. Currently adoption is not allowed by two people living in a partnership. In such instances, the courts will make an adoption order to one individual of the partnership, provided the usual approval has taken place. The other partner can then apply for a residence order. Such arrangements are possible but still unusual.

Guardians have a right of access to social service records and adoption files. This provide an opportunity to assess how far the schedule 2 report is consistent with what has been written in those records. The order in which people are seen, that is the child, the adopters, the parents, the social service staff may vary depending on the situation. During their investigation the guardian may come across something not sufficiently explored, such as a relative showing interest in the child, but this information never reached the adoption panel. At the same time, guardians need to be wary not to stir up a settled situation unless this is likely to lead to a different outcome. Guardians need to discuss the adoption with children who are aware of the situation and old enough to understand. These children must be seen on their own.

If a guardian finds that a parent is willing to consent after all, then the guardian needs to contact the court and obtain authorisation to be appointed as a reporting officer. It has been known for a guardian to be appointed as a reporting officer for one parent who consents to the adoption and a guardian to the other who is unwilling.

There are situations where the guardian needs to think whether an adoption order is the right way forward. This may be particularly applicable for older children, who will have contact with their parents and where a residence order, (Section 8 order under the Children Act), may be more appropriate. Another situation which has given cause for concern is the placement of children outside their racial and cultural groups. For example the placement of an Asian child who comes from a Muslim family into a white Christian family would not be considered appropriate or good practice. Although most agencies have developed clear guidelines on not placing children outside their own cultural and racial groups, there could be an instances where a black child has been placed with a white family. This may arise, because the black child was placed with the white family initially when a baby and as a short term measure. Because of drift and lack of decision, the child has made attachments so that moving him/her would create considerable distress and emotional damage. In such situations the guardian has to take a pragmatic approach. Guardians need to consider the three pivotal placement features of attachment, identity and survival skills. In other instances, in order to gain sufficient confidence and sense of identity, a particular child may have to be moved from a white to a black family.

3. THE GUARDIAN AND SPECIAL SITUATIONS

PARENTS WITH MENTAL HEALTH PROBLEMS

In cases where it is clear that the parent is not able to give consent because of their mental health problems, the guardian should ensure that the case is transferred to the High Court, by writing to the court from which the appointment was made. The transfer would then enable the Official Solicitor to act on behalf of the parent who is unable to give instruction or give consent.

PROTECTED CHILDREN

Adoption of this group of children means that they have not been placed with their adopters by an adoption agency. This applies to the following groups:

A) STEP-PARENT ADOPTIONS

In this category, a birth parent and step-parent applies as a married couple to adopt the child, thus removing parental responsibility from the other birth parent. Guardians need to be aware of the implications of this; though such a step may provide more security for a child, it can also create difficulties about contact with the divorced parent and other siblings about inheritance. Such an adoption involves the natural parent who has remarried in adopting their own child and needing to give consent to the adoption order. This is a situation the proposed new adoption laws had hoped to regulate. The adopted child may well have a view about the adoption and must be interviewed if old enough to express a view.

B) ADOPTION BY FOSTERPARENTS OR PRIVATE FOSTERPARENTS

Applications can be made once these individuals have looked after a child for twelve months. Support may not be obtained from the local authority who may oppose the application. Vigilance is necessary particularly in cases of private fostering to ensure that the placement of a child was not by a "third party" which is now illegal. All the time the rights of the child and birth parents must be borne in mind.

C) INTER-COUNTRY ADOPTION

This is increasingly a complex area, involving considerations of culture, of entrance visas of different national adoption legislation, of ensuring that the correct documentation is available and ascertaining who was responsible for arranging it in the first place. In practice, inter-country adoptions fall into adoptions:

- organised throughout by a responsible government authorised agency overseas, assisted by a local authority in the UK;
- adoptions arranged privately by the adopters overseas but with the help of the local authority in the UK;
- adoptions arranged privately by adopters overseas with no official intervention;
- adoptions by a relative or friend of the child or his family.

If an adoption has taken place in the country of origin of the child, the guardian must ensure that the adoption of that country is recognised here, otherwise an adoption would have to take place here. The guardian must ensure that there is documentation to prove that the parents of the child gave their agreement willingly. If a child has been brought into the country without a visa, then the Home Office may need to be asked if they wished to become party to the proceedings. In any case, application must be made to the Home Office if an adopter wishes to adopt a child who is not a British citizen. Other complicating features concern illegal payments to individuals to obtain children for adoption. The delayed adoption legislation had intended to address many of the concerns that surround inter-country adoption in order to simplify and clarify matters.

4. CONTACT IN ADOPTION

This has been an increasing trend in the last five years, with an emphasis on more openness and less secrecy. A number of adoption agencies encourage adopters to meet birth parents before the adoption takes place to provide some first hand information about themselves. Many adoption orders have agreements which include indirect contact whereby there is an exchange of letter, cards and photographs between the adopted child(ren) and their birth families once or twice a year through the adoption agency. Continued face to face contact is still rare although it can occur on a regular basis once an adoption order has been made. There is increasing recognition that for some children continuing contact will sustain their identity. The courts, however, have decreed that contact cannot be imposed on the adopters but can only take place with their agreement. Guardians should always consider this issue and check that it has been contemplated by the placement agency. Direct contact can either be written into the adoption order if the applicants agree, or sought as a separate contact order or there is an agreement by the parties concerned.

5. FREEING FOR ADOPTION

This procedure was implemented in 1984. It was intended to save time when placing babies for adoption on the assumption that once agreement has been obtained for a freeing order from the parent, the adopters would not become involved in the process. In practice, freeing takes as long if the order is contested. The issues for the

guardian are in main similar to those in adoption, but the
following points should be noted:

- only an adoption agency can apply for a freeing order;
- the matter must have been considered by the adoption panel
- prospective adopters must be available;
- the agency must provide a statement of facts, giving the
  sequence of events leading to the application for a freeing order;
- if the child is in care, the application does not require parental
  agreement. The order can be contested by the parents, with the
  court having to decide whether to dispense with their agreement;
- if the child is not in care, then at least one of the parents must
  consent to the application.

The order lapses if the child has not been placed with
adopters within twelve months of its making. Guardians
need to discuss with birth parents whether they wish to be
involved again if a placement has not taken place within a
year.

6. THE GUARDIAN AND THE COURTS

The guardian is expected to advise the court whether the
child should attend for the hearing. Older children are
expected to attend their adoption, while younger children
are excused. However, discretion must be exercised if the
adoption is contested as in those instances it would be
wiser to keep the children away from the courts.
Alternatively, the guardian can arrange for a split hearing,
so that the order can be made at a different date form the
consideration of disputed issues and the child can meet
the judge. Experience shows that children and their
adopted families benefit from a sense of celebration and
ceremony about the adoption. Guardians should be pro-
active in promoting this.

The guardian has to submit a report on their findings
and recommendations. Unlike reports in care proceedings,
this is usually a confidential document unless the court has
given leave for its distribution to the parties. Reports
should be written in such a way that different people can
read the parts relating to them without having to read the
whole report. This in itself should be discriminating in not

repeating information already in the schedule 2 report. If there is different or conflicting material, this needs to be brought to the court's attention.

7. THE TASK OF REPORTING OFFICER

The tasks are laid out in the 1984 adoption rules. For the parents, meeting the reporting officer is the last chance to reconsider the adoption or to voice any disquiet about the proceedings.

In essence the reporting officer must:

- witness a willing parent's signature agreeing to the adoption;
- ensure that agreement has been freely given;
- ensure that the parent knows what is involved before signing the form;
- see the child's birth certificate
- in freeing cases confirm that the parent has been given an opportunity or making a declaration not to be involved in future questions concerning their child;
- write a report for the court.

As in an adoption, reporting officers should not start their task without the schedule 2 report being available. Documentation similar to that required by the guardian ad litem, should also be sent by the court. If the parents refuse to sign their agreement to the adoption, this must be reported to the court with the latter appointing the reporting officer as guardian in a contested adoption. The report accompanying the signed form needs to be brief but is confidential to the court.

The guardian and the legal system

This chapter is concerned with the guardian's role within the legal framework of the Children Act, their relationship and responsibilities towards the courts, and their working arrangements with the child's solicitor. The main section deals with care proceedings under the Children Act 1989. The last section deals with the guardian's working relationship with solicitors under the Adoption Act 1976.

PROCEEDINGS UNDER THE CHILDREN ACT

The guardian's role as defined by legislation is seen as one of collaboration with the courts. Guardians are expected to inform the courts, usually through the clerk to the court, of any unusual development, or change in the time table. In care courts or the High Courts, contact has to be made through the clerk to the judges or the relevant listing office in the court. Guardians should be pro-active, take the initiative; this means instructing the solicitors to carry out a specific task. This may mean asking for a directions hearing, drawing the court's attention to other individuals who should be involved or should be considered as parties to the proceedings. Guardians are accountable for their opinions and actions to the courts alone.

1. APPOINTING A SOLICITOR FOR THE CHILD

The Family Proceedings Rules 1991 which govern the way the Children Act is implemented, deal with the appointment of solicitors to represent children. The latter can be appointed either by the court or by the guardian who has been appointed to the case. Generally there is an expectation that solicitors should be appointed by the guardian on the basis that some specific selection may be necessary; an adolescent who has been sexually abused may find it easier to talk to a woman solicitor, or there may be a question of ethnicity or other specific knowledge. Although not mandatory, solicitors should be selected from the Children Panel list issued by the Law Society, as this will indicate some level of experience and practice.

Having appointed a solicitor, usually by telephone, the guardian and solicitor should meet to discuss how the work is going to be approached and shared. In order to be able to do this, both need to have information about the case being brought to court. It is usually the solicitor's responsibility to obtain the local authority's application form and supporting statement from the local authority. Often proceedings are brought where there is little time between the appointment of a guardian and the first hearing, so that the guardian is unlikely to be in a position to take a specific stance or oppose the application.

When approaching a solicitor, guardians should make a determined effort to appoint a wide range of solicitors and thus not risk developing a collusive relationship. Equally they are in a powerful position to encourage less experienced solicitors to increase their experience and skills.

2. WORKING WITH THE CHILD'S SOLICITOR

Once appointed, the solicitor must apply for legal aid on behalf of the child. This is usually granted automatically, but occasionally delays occur. The first meeting between guardian and solicitor should cover a number of aspects and include the following:

- whether the present court is an appropriate level for hearing of the case;
- listing possible witnesses and discussing which people the guardian is going to interview;
- discussing possible expert evidence which may be needed
- whether any interviews should be carried out together – here the guardian needs to be aware that it is not professionally appropriate for the child's solicitor to interview parents without their legal representative being present;
- at which stage the solicitor will see the child (children), alone or in conjunction with the guardian. Solicitors should always see the children they represent at least once, regardless of age or understanding;
- an assurance from the solicitor, that he will deal with all aspects of the case personally. If unexpected difficulties occur about a court attendance, such as directions hearing he will inform the guardian in order to discuss how to deal with this. It may be that a colleague will act as a substitute or the solicitor will need to brief counsel. In either case, the guardian must be consulted;
- an agreement that all letters the solicitor writes on behalf of the guardian and child are copied to the guardian.

In order to safeguard children's interests, it is important that the guardian and solicitor maintain a close working relationship throughout the case. For the guardian, such a relationship will often be the main source of support and an opportunity for consultation and sharing of views. At the same time, the court makes it clear that the children's solicitor is required to act in accordance with the instructions of the guardian. It is not open to the solicitor to reject these and simply proceed with the case independently. The solicitor should refer to the guardian for guidance. If there is a disagreement between solicitor and guardian about the conduct of the case, and the matter cannot be resolved between them, then this must be referred back to the court for guidance.

3. Separation from the child's solicitor and termination of solicitor's appointment

Occasionally conflict between the guardian and solicitor may arise. This is likely to occur with older children who are deemed to be able to give their solicitor instructions independently. It may happen that a child has been badly abused at home, the guardian does not think it in the child's interest that he should return there, but the child disagrees with this opinion. In such an event, the matter should be returned to the court, for a directions hearing to consider separate representation for the guardian, who will then have to appoint a solicitor for themselves. Most panel managers would wish to know about such developments in order to ensure that the local authority concerned are aware of the court directions, as the local authority will then have to become responsible for the fees for the new solicitor for the guardian.

The age when a child is able to give instructions independently is not always clear-cut. It is crucial that the child's understanding is judged on the basis of his comprehension of the issues. This should be considered with children aged ten or upwards. Although chronological age plays a part, other factors are also relevant. This applies particularly to children who exhibit emotional disturbances which affect their judgement and who in spite of their chronological age are deemed not to be able to instruct a solicitor. Judgement about this issue, as determined by the court rules, has to be left to the solicitor concerned, whose job it is to decide whether he can take instruction from a particular child.

On rare occasions, the guardian may feel unable to sustain a collaborative relationship with the child's solicitor. The court rules allow for the termination of the solicitor's appointment on the application of the guardian, who will have to make an application to the court for this to take place.

4. ATTENDING INTERIM AND DIRECTIONS' HEARINGS

In those instances, where the court makes an interim care or supervision order, these will be renewed at four weekly intervals. The rules allow for one eight week interval period during one proceedings. In general, if there is no disagreement about the continuation of the order, then only the local authority need to turn up in court for the renewal. Occasionally interim orders may be contested by parents, sometimes by the guardian, although the latter is likely to be rare. If there is a contest at an interim stage, often about whether children should remain in care, the guardian may be directed to provide a report and attend the hearing.

In those cases where there is an application for care, but no interim orders are made, the proceedings will continue interspersed by directions hearings.

The court rules state that all parties must attend directions' hearings, in addition guardians are expected to be available, although not parties to the proceedings, as their presence is often crucial. If for some reason they are unable to be present, they are required to obtain court permission to be excused. This is usually by the solicitor via clerk to the court, magistrates or judges in the county courts. Before a directions hearing takes place, the guardian and the child's solicitor should consult as to whether they wish to seek any directions or clarification from the court – they may wish to point out that certain statements or reports which were due had not been received. Sometimes there are difficulties in getting experts' reports in time, or completing assessments.

All these factors should be brought to the notice of the court, so that the latter is able to maintain a grip on the

proceedings and deal with the preliminary issues before
the final hearing.

5. PREPARATION FOR THE FINAL HEARING

Before the final hearing takes place, and before the
guardian's final report is written, the guardian and
solicitor should have a detailed discussion about the likely
recommendation and outcome of the case. They should
discuss the nature and weight of the evidence, the
availability of witnesses, of documents and statements.
They should cover appraisal of the local authority's views,
and the areas likely to be contentious and where
differences may emerge.

Once the guardian has completed her report and
clarified her recommendations, further discussions with
the solicitor should take place to consider differences and
how these are likely to be dealt with by the courts. By then
the solicitor and guardian will probably have a fairly clear
idea whether the hearing is likely to be contested by any of
the parties involved. The guardian's views will have been
conveyed through her report to the parties, so that they
too will be appraised as to whether the matter will be
contested or there is room for accommodation. If the
parties come from a different ethnic group and there are
language difficulties, the guardian or the parents' solicitor
should ensure that interpreters are available for the
hearing. This can often prolong the length of the court
hearing.

Increasingly, guardians are being encouraged by courts
to see whether matters can be resolved by agreement
rather than by several days in contested hearings.
Sometimes these cannot be avoided and justice demands
that evidence is heard and tested. The guardian has an
important role in determining how the final hearing is to
be managed; suggesting to the child's solicitor that
producing a list of facts which are agreed by the parties is
one way of reducing the contest and adversarial
proceedings.

6. GIVING EVIDENCE

The guardian and solicitor or counsel must attend the final
hearing. The guardian must be prepared to give evidence

and justify the stance she has taken on behalf of the child. If the proceedings are likely to be contentious, it is useful to rehearse the main issues on which the guardian is likely to be questioned with the solicitor. If for instance, the issue at stake is contact between parents and children, then the guardian must substantiate her argument. In many instances, deciding on the frequency of contact is a matter of trial and error rather than some intrinsic knowledge; courts appreciate it if guardians are straightforward about such matters and acknowledge the basis for their recommendations.

7. ATTENDANCE OF CHILDREN AT HEARINGS

Although the child is a party to the proceedings, the court rules provide that the proceedings can take place in the absence of the child concerned. There are in fact differences of view as to whether children should attend hearings. In the main, children have been discouraged from attending courts in care proceedings and professionals are frequently reminded that it should not be routine practice for children to come to hearings. Older children are more easily accommodated in magistrates courts, than county or the High Court. Guardians are however urged to think carefully before making arrangements for children to attend. Areas about which there is less contention are either where the child has given his own instructions or where the court has been asked to make a secure accommodation order and the hearings are about the curtailment of liberty for the child.

8. WITHDRAWING PROCEEDINGS

There are a number of cases, where the proceedings in themselves have affected desired or required changes, and where the local authority has developed a good enough working relationship with the parent(s) to enable the care plan with no order to be implemented. In such instances, the local authority may consider that to continue with their application could be counterproductive for the achievement of the desired aims. The Act allows for the withdrawal of proceedings, provided leave has been sought from the court. The party who seeks the withdrawal has to serve the other parties in writing giving their reasons. The court can grant this written request, but must give the guardian an opportunity to make representations. If the guardian indicates her reservation to the withdrawal, then there must be a hearing. Even in those instances, where all the parties agree for the withdrawal of the proceedings, the court clerk, or judge is still entitled to insist on a hearing for adjudication.

Alternatively, the application to withdraw proceedings can be done orally, provided the guardian is present in court and provided the parties have been warned beforehand of this proposal.

PROCEEDINGS UNDER THE ADOPTION ACT

Solicitors only feature in adoptions, where the child is made a party to the adoption proceedings, as is the rule in High Court adoptions, or the guardian requests the county court that she be made a party to the proceedings. The latter may be a necessary step, where there are complex issues, where the case is vigorously contested by the parent(s), where expert witness evidence is being sought or there are procedural matters which require the services of a lawyer.

In High Court adoptions, the relationship with the solicitor is not dissimilar to that of care proceedings. In county court adoptions, the solicitor represents the guardian, if the latter is made a party.

The guardian, administration and report writing

This chapter considers the administrative tasks involved in the work of the guardian, the structure of reports and the principles underlying these.

1. THE GUARDIAN AND ADMINISTRATION

Increasingly, guardians are expected to keep comprehensive records on their cases, records of interviews, plans for future action, time sheets to indicate how time has been spent, information about details of the child's family, and a great many other documents and papers. The days when a few notes were kept on the back of an envelope have long disappeared. There is an expectation that files must be kept in a confidential place where others do not have access. This applies to guardians whether self-employed or working from local authority or other agency premises. The need to keep accurate records of interviews is borne out in situations where guardians are asked specific questions in evidence as to what was said to them on a particular day and by whom. Guardians must keep letters received, in date order and any response which was made.

2. THE MAIN FUNCTION OF THE GUARDIAN'S REPORT

The main purpose is to inform and guide the court on the child's future disposition. The guardian is asked not only to represent the child's interests, but to produce a well argued and convincing account of what those interests are. This must highlight and tease out the relevant issues in the case and in the child's life, balance these, and with an eye to the future, guardians must make a recommendation.

The report must be a demonstration and end result of the way the guardian has gone about the job of investigating, of making an assessment and the way the conclusions have been reached. In essence, the report should unfold like a good detective story; if well argued and logically presented, the document will not come as a surprise. It will be read by all the parties to the proceedings and should be understandable, free from jargon or patronage. We are aware that in many courts at whatever level, the first thing a judge or magistrate will do is turn to the guardian's report. This reinforces the expectation, that the report should be self contained, should not rely extensively on other documentation or refer the reader continuously to other reports and statements and should stand by itself. The assumptions sometimes made that to repeat history or other factual material is superfluous, are not valid.

It has to be remembered that reports are written with a view to presenting the findings to the court and with the outcome of the case in mind. It is composed before all the evidence has been heard, and should not be taken as the guardian's last word. There are times when the guardian may wish to add to the conclusions or even rethink them if other evidence is presented to the court. There are of course situations where no evidence is heard, as by the time the hearing date arrives, there is a large amount of agreement as to the outcome of the proceedings. But even in those instances guardians may shift their position, because of fresh information.

3. ESSENTIALS OF A REPORT

Reports should be typed in double spacing, pages numbered and paragraphs separately numbered. Guardians are appointed to a variety of proceedings, so therefore reports cannot all follow the same format. Where the focus of the enquiry is narrow, such as a child assessment order, or a change in contact arrangements, the report may be shorter to cover these particular issues. Reports should not repeat large chunks of history, yet there should be enough background information to give a comprehensive picture of the situation. It is very important to distinguish between opinion and fact, giving sources for both these aspects. If the report for the final hearing is not the first prepared by the guardian, it is advisable to recommend that this report needs to be read in conjunction with an earlier report. Most importantly reports must have a structure which is easy to follow.

4. CONTENTS OF THE REPORT.

The following format has been found to be useful and is therefore reproduced with some explanation as to the meaning of the headings. It is mainly applicable for care proceedings but could be amended for other kinds of hearings.

● **Front page**

The front page must indicate what kind of proceedings are being brought, by whom, the name of the child, the court, and the local authority bringing the proceedings. Dates of children's birth, of final or interim hearing, of guardian's appointment to the case must also be recorded as well as date of the report. It must also provide a reminder of the confidentiality of the report.

● **The guardian's qualification and experience**

● **Nature of proceedings**

This includes a brief summary of the nature of the proceedings, and who is bringing them; who is involved in terms of parties, previous hearings, details of directions given, appointment of expert witnesses, who has parental responsibility.

● **Family structure**

This should give details of the child's and family members' history, names, occupation and dates of birth. Ethnicity, language and religion details are useful here, as well as living accommodation for the family. Sometimes a family tree or geneogram might help.

● **Sources of information and inquiries made by the guardian**

This should be divided into four sections:

a) people who have been interviewed and dates. This should include details of where the child has been interviewed, whether seen alone, and whether the child has been seen with members of his family. Indicate if significant people could not be seen;

b) Documents and reports read with date if applicable, but do not list all documents read in social service files. If significant information has come to light, then the court's attention needs to be drawn to this;

c) list reports from experts appointed;

d) list the people spoken to on the telephone, the child's solicitor need not be included in this.

▶

● **Events leading to the proceedings**

Brief outline of key events leading to the proceedings is useful indicating the catalyst which led to the application.

● **A synopsis of the family background**

This should include the important events in the child's life, and provide an overview of the child's setting. Sources of information should be stated.

● **The child**

Here it is useful to give a description of the child, including how she or he is seen by others. This must include reference to language, sex, background, religion, race and culture, and any disabilities. An assessment is required of the child's physical, emotional and educational needs. Similarly, an assessment must be made of the child's key relationships, attachment to members inside and outside the family. There should be comment on any harm the child has suffered or is likely to suffer in the future. The above does not need to be set out in the form of the checklist, but if the above topics have been covered, then the welfare checklist has been addressed.

● **The child's wishes and feelings**

The wishes and feelings of the child which can be established should be stated separately. Where possible a direct quote from the child is useful. This depends on the child's understanding and age. In case of very young children, it may be difficult to elicit what the child wants or feels. The child's reactions to placement, contact with parents and siblings can give clues to his relationships and feelings. It is important that courts are given information on this aspect.

● **Assessment of parents as carers**

The views given by those who have parental responsibility and of the parents about the children's' future must be elicited. An assessment must be made of their capacities to meet the child's varied needs and any support they require in order to achieve this. Additionally, comment should be made as to whether such support is realistically forthcoming. If formal rehabilitation programmes have taken place, these should be commented on.

◀

● **Local authority involvement and future plans**

This section should be a critical appraisal of the local authority's involvement with the family, what provisions have been made in the past, what proceedings have been taken Comments on good practice and appropriate services having been provided should be included. Appraisal of the care plan is required here

● **The child's contact with parents and wider family**

Information should be given about whom the child is seeing, how frequently, where and how this has worked in practice. Other comments should be addressed as to the local authority's efforts to promote contact and what future plans about this are likely to be.

● **Discussion and assessment**

This section provides an opportunity for the guardian to summarise and comment on their findings and highlight particular concerns or issues for the court. If there are going to be any changes in the child's circumstances, this section would be a useful place to discuss these. This section provides an opportunity to show what the guardian's investigation has produced. If research findings are particularly useful, they can be quoted and properly referenced in this part of the report. Most courts tend to fight shy of too many research references, preferring instead observations coupled with experience and background knowledge in the field.

The welfare checklist could be summarised here very briefly.

● **Options available to the court**

This should spell out clearly the range of powers available to the court, and that the court must consider whether an order is better than no order.

The different orders available, including section 8 orders, (prohibited steps order, specific issues, contact) should be listed, considered individually and information provided as to why one order is more appropriate than another.

● **Recommendations**

The recommendation must be clearly stated.

● **Reports must be signed and dated**

5. DISTRIBUTION AND USE OF THE REPORT

Although the rules state that guardian reports in care proceedings should be filed with the court and other parties a week before the hearing most courts, when timetabling proceedings, direct a lengthier period before the final hearing. These directions must be adhered to. If for some reason, a guardian is unable to comply with the court's direction, a letter of explanation must be written to the court.

Normally, the guardian should discuss the report with the solicitor, the parents or other parties to the proceedings, the child, if old enough and of sufficient understanding, and the local authority. There are no specific rules about the child being entitled to a copy of the report. Whether to show it to the child or talk about its contents is a matter for the judgement of the solicitor and guardian. To no one should the recommendation come as a surprise, as guardians should keep others in touch with their thinking.

The distribution of the report is the task of the court, but in many areas, this has been taken over by the child's solicitor, who is responsible for its distribution. The report, along with other documents, is usually read by judges and magistrates before the proceedings begin. The report itself is confidential and must not be reproduced, without permission of the court.

6. OTHER REPORTS

INTERIM REPORTS

Frequently, courts ask the guardian to write an interim report on some specific issue or topic. At times this has to be done within a short space of time. The reasons for such a task are numerous, they can be concerned with contact between child and parent, or in a complex case, the stage which the case has reached.

In other instances, there could be a change in direction because something has happened, such as the local authority seeking an interim care order, where children have remained at home from the beginning of proceedings.

> **Case example**
>
> Agnes and Mary had remained at home with their parents, although the local authority had taken proceedings mainly because they were out of control at home. Following visits to the home both by the social worker and guardian at different times, it became apparent, that the inability of the parents to exercise adequate control over their activities posed dangers for them. A decision was taken by the local authority to apply for an interim care order. Directions were sought for timetabling of statements. The guardian was directed to write an interim report which commented on the need to remove these children from home and what programme could be proposed for them.

ADOPTION REPORTS

Inevitably their emphasis has to be different. The basic information on the front sheet would be similar to that for care proceedings. This could then be followed as suggested below.

> ● **Proceedings before the court**
> Details of the adoption application, a brief summary of earlier hearings in the courts and orders made.
>
> ● **Family structure of birth parents**
> This would give details of the child's natural family.
>
> ● **Family structure of applicants**
> And similar identifying details.
>
> ● **Details of placement**
> This would include when the child was placed with the adopters, when they were approved, whether this is an agency adoption or not.
>
> ● **Sources of information and listing of all documents seen**
> This needs to list files of adoption agency, social service files, schedule 2 report.
> There needs to be an an account of who was seen with dates, and a list of people spoken to on the telephone.
>
> ● **Brief history of the case**
> This should not repeat information provided in the schedule 2 report. Comments can be made about this if relevant. ▶

- **Details of the child**

This should include matters relating to race, culture, language, disabilities and a description of the child.

- **Wishes and feelings of the child**

This area may not always be fully recorded as it depends on the age of the child and how much he is aware as to what is happening. Comments about existing and future views on contact should be mentioned here.

- **The applicants**

Although the schedule 2 report will cover this, a brief statement about their involvement with the child and their commitment to it should be commented on. Similarly consideration should be given as to the suitability of the applicants in terms of race, gender, culture and religion.

- **The birth family**

This section should consider whether the parent or parents are withholding their consent unreasonably to the proposed adoption or freeing process.

- **The work of the agency in planning for the child**

Guardians need to consider the work of the agency in terms of practice and policy and how they carried out the work in relation to the adoption.

- **The guardian's assessment**

This should include an assessment of the child and a statement as to whether the order sought, or any other, such as a residence order, might be more suitable. Consideration must be given to direct or indirect contact.

- **The options available to the court**

The guardian needs to consider whether an adoption order is in the best interests of the child, and if the parents do not agree whether they are unreasonable in withholding their consent. The guardian should also address whether a section 8 order might be more suitable. This could well be the case in step-parent adoption.

- **Recommendations**

These should be clearly stated. The report must be signed and dated.

The guardian and other proceedings

This chapter briefly summarises other law proceedings for which guardians may be appointed.

1. THE HUMAN FERTILISATION AND EMBRYOLOGY ACT 1990

The Human Fertilisation and Embryology Act 1990 provides for the appointment of guardians in applications for a parental order on a child born through a surrogacy agreement. Parental orders as per Section 30 of the Act come within the ambit of family proceedings. This means that Section 8 and Section 37 of the Children Act apply. In Section 8 the court can consider residence orders, prohibited steps and specific issue orders along with contact orders. Section 37 means that the court can order the local authority to make an investigation and report as to whether care proceedings should be initiated. The guardian has to have regard for the checklist of Section 1(1)(a) and 1 (2) of the Children Act. Guardians are advised to keep abreast of developments in the code of practice of the HFE Authority. One of the Authority's key task is to license clinics, keep records and various registers and maintain or update the code of practice.

A) ESSENTIALS OF SECTION 30 ORDERS

The legal position of a child born as a result of a surrogacy agreement is that the mother who gives birth is the child's mother in all respects. The birth father is the father of the child. In order for a Section 30 application to succeed, the following must apply:

- The child is to be carried by a woman other than the wife of the donor father;
- There has to be a genetic relationship with at least one of the commissioning parents;
- An application has to be made within six months of the birth of the child; ▶

> ◀
> - At least one of the parents must be domiciled in the United Kingdom and the child's home must be with the commissioning parents;
> - The commissioning parents must be married to each other and must be over the age of 18;
> - The conception was only by artificial method.

As a result of the parental order, the parental responsibility of the birth mother is terminated as in adoption.

Guardians should note that a parental order does not confer UK nationality on the child.

B) MAKING AN APPLICATION

An application can be lodged with the court, (usually family proceedings courts) as soon as the child is placed with the commissioning parents, but agreement cannot be given until the child is six weeks old.

Once an application is lodged with the court if the surrogate mother changes her mind, the child cannot be returned without leave of the court.

Once an application is lodged, the court must appoint a guardian ad litem.

C) THE TASK OF THE GUARDIAN AD LITEM

The duties of the guardian are similar to those in adoption proceedings. She must see documents such as a marriage certificate and birth certificate of the child. The child is not a party to the proceedings and the guardian is not legally represented unless the matter is heard in the High Court. The Official Solicitor can be helpful in these situations.

There is nothing equivalent to a Schedule 2 report as obtained in adoption. Instead, the guardian receives two forms, one the originating application from the commissioning parents, and the other from the respondent birth parent.

Guardians should not start any investigation until they have the minimum amount of information in their possession.

The task of the guardian falls into the following:

- ensuring that the agreement of the birth parent is given unconditionally, and with a full understanding of its implications. This will involve interviewing the birth parent and married spouse if she has one. If the mother is in a stable relationship, it would be advisable to meet her partner;
- the guardian has to ensure that only reasonable expenses have been incurred. The legislation does not give guidance on this. Loss of earnings, food, clothes, travel costs fall into this category. Making judgements about this aspect may be difficult for guardians who have no right of access to key information. They can check with the applicants and surrogate mother, what payments were made, as the court has to be satisfied that no money or benefit (other than acceptable expenses) has passed between parties before making an order;
- the guardian has to be aware of the general circumstances in which the agreement has been given. If registered clinics have been used, then there is often an opportunity for the parties to meet and some counselling to have taken place. However, not all surrogacy agreements are made through a registered clinic. This would then imply that guardians will have to find out what method of conception was used;
- agreement can be given orally or in writing. Usually it is done in writing, although there is no statutory form. Guardians would be advised to obtain the surrogate mother's agreement in writing;
- at present there is no upper age limit for commissioning parents, and although guardians may have concerns about this, it would be difficult not to recommend an order on this basis alone;
- there is advice in the code of practice that guardians should obtain information on other children in the applicants' family. There could be difficulties in this, as the guardian has no standing where other children are concerned, cannot interview them without their parents' permission and the whole issue of explaining her role is inevitably raised. This is in contrast to good practice in adoption, where other children in the family are seen on the basis that family secrets can be divisive and not helpful;
- although the code does not advise this, guardians should contact the local social service department as to whether the applicants or surrogate parent are known to them. Furthermore there is no power to obtain police records. Guardians are not required to

▶

◀

make a thorough investigation of the applicants, and will need all
their skills to ensure within one or two interviews there is nothing
untoward about the applicants;
● if after making her investigation, the guardian is of the opinion
that a Section 30 order should not be made, then she must
advise the court of this.

D) THE REPORT FROM THE GUARDIAN

Although there is no proforma at present, guardians will
have to include in their report, reasons for the surrogacy
and attitudes of the applicants about telling the child in
due course about their origins. Other areas to be covered,
include the other children in the family, information about
the commissioning parents, information about the
surrogate parent, the expenses involved, and what options
the court has regarding this order. If the guardian is
satisfied that the court should make this order, then there
should be a clear recommendation stating this.

2. THE FAMILY LAW REFORM ACT 1996

Part IV of the act came into force on 1 October 1997.
Guardians will have have a role in this. Applications in
which domestic violence and/or occupation of the family
home are a feature, will inevitably have some impact on
the task of the guardian. Courts will now have the power
to make an exclusion order attached to an interim care
order or final order. Guardians would be expected to
comment on such proposals. Similarly exclusion orders
can be attached to emergency protection orders, so that a
particular person is excluded from the home in the
interests of the child.

Section 52 and Schedule 6 add new provisions to the
Children Act 1989. This section sets out conditions which
must be satisfied. These include requirements such that
there is reasonable cause to believe that if a person is
excluded from the house where the child lives, the child
will cease to suffer significant harm and that another
person in the house is available to give to the child
reasonable care and consents to the exclusion agreement.
The court may attach a power of arrest to the exclusion
requirement.

Epilogue

> *"Guardians are in an almost unique position to evaluate the care received by children who are reliant on the support of the local authority in order to receive adequate parenting... Guardians are not also bound by any loyalties to the local authority, and charged with seeking the best outcome of the child... A weakness of the position of the guardian service as a knowledgeable inspector of local authority child care services is that guardians make a series of individual judgements, with no attempts to apply common standards of individual good practice."*
> ***(Bury, Oldham & Rochdale GALRO Panel evidence to the DOH, the Guardian ad Litem and Reporting Officer Service, an overview, DOH 1995).***

The current move towards some degree of standardisation (*Implementing National Standards, a Guide through Quality Assurance for the Guardian Service*, DOH 1997) is seeking to deal with the latter issue. It arouses opposition from many guardians and panels, as it seems to threaten their autonomy and permission to make an independent, individual assessment and judgement about the merits of the case.

Guardians are divided about the kind and level of oversight they find acceptable and from whom. Like everyone else, we work in a situation of increasing financial constraint and control, and are subject to the same professional frustration and anxiety as the gap between expectations and resources widens.

In our view, like everything else, the work of the guardian requires a balance; in this case, between individualism and omnipotence. One of the great attractions of the job is the opportunity to operate more freely than in any other social work position and to be taken seriously professionally and afforded a kind of expert status and power. In the early days of the service, guardians could develop fairly idiosyncratically and were only accountable in a rather abstract manner to the courts, or, via the complaint system, to their panel manager.

Increasingly, there has been a move towards the broad standardisation of report format and the content of investigation, and to some control over conditions of service and hours spent working on cases. Famously, the Cornwall guardians successfully resisted in the courts their authority's attempt to set a statutory limit on time charged per case. In 1997 some Inner London guardians successfully challenged legally their panel's right to insist on limiting the number of panels a guardian could belong to

For some, the job is losing its lure and there are fears that it will become over-identified with the financial and ideological power of local authorities and will lose its unique force as the unrestrained "voice of the child", the idea born out of the painful experience in the 1970s of Maria Colwell going unheard when she was returned home to her death.

The authors believe it will be possible to find a balance between our right to investigate and recommend freely, to speak for the child clearly, and the right of the state and community in which we operate to expect a reliable and consistent service which can be questioned as rigorously as we probe the operations of other professionals.

It remains an absorbing and useful role; operating on several boundaries – between the legal and welfare worlds, between notions of "proof" and "opinion", and above all on the boundary between the child and the world he or she inhabits.

Appendix I:
The welfare checklist

SECTION 1 (3) CHILDREN ACT 1989

The court should have regard in particular to:
   a) the ascertainable wishes and feelings of the child concerned
      (considered in the light of his age and understanding);
   b) his physical, emotional and educational needs;
   c) the likely effect on him of any change in his circumstances;
   d) his age, sex, background and any characteristic of his which
      the court considers relevant;
   e) any harm he has suffered or is at risk of suffering;
   f) how capable each of his parents, and any other person in
      relation to whom the court considers the question to be
      relevant, is of meeting his needs;
   g) the range of powers available to the court under this Act in the
      proceedings in question.

SECTION 4

   a) the court is considering whether to make, vary or discharge a
      Section 8 order, and the making, variation or discharge of the
      order is opposed by any party to the proceedings, or;
   b) the court is considering whether to make, vary or discharge
      an order under Part IV;
   c) where the court is considering whether or not to make one or
      more order under this Act with respect to a child, it shall not
      make the order unless it considers that doing so would be
      better for the child than making no order at all.

Appendix II:
National standards for the guardian ad litem

Department of Health and Welsh Office 1995

STANDARDS 1-3

These are concerned with the management of the GAL panels and have been excluded in this appendix.

WELFARE OF THE CHILD (STANDARD 4)

The guardian ensures that the welfare of the child is the paramount consideration; in adoption cases, the guardian safeguards the interests of the child.

THE CHILD'S WISHES AND FEELINGS (STANDARD 5)

Full consideration is given to ascertaining both the wishes and feelings of the child.

THE GUARDIAN'S INDEPENDENCE AND IMPARTIALITY (STANDARD 6)

The guardian is professionally independent from other parties and works impartially with parents, other family members, carers and professionals at all stages in the process, subject to the need to ensure the welfare of the child.

UNPREJUDICED AND SENSITIVE PRACTICE (STANDARD 7)

In their work with children and families, guardians positively respond to issues associated with gender, race, culture, religious language and disability.

THE NEED FOR A COMPETENT INVESTIGATION (STANDARD 8)

The investigation is undertaken in a competent manner; having been appointed, the guardian constructs an initial plan setting out the intended work programme and proceeds to implement it with minimum delay, updating as necessary.

WELFARE CHECKLIST (STANDARD 9)

Where this is statutorily required, the guardian's investigation incorporates the checklist of the Children Act.

EVALUATION OF INFORMATION (STANDARD 10)

Having brought together the relevant information, the guardian evaluates it and makes judgements about what future arrangements will be in the best interests of the child, whether any order is needed and if it is, whether the order sought is the one most likely to achieve the child's best interests.

REPORT FORMAT (STANDARD 11)

The guardian's report accords with national and local guidelines on report writing.

ATTENDING DIRECTIONS APPOINTMENTS AND COURT HEARINGS (STANDARD 12)

The guardian attends direction appointments in accordance with the court rules and is prepared for each court hearing.

CLOSURE OF CASES (STANDARD 13)

Prior to closing a case, the guardian needs to ensure that appropriate action has been considered and if necessary carried out in respect of the child.

RESPONSIBILITY OF PANEL MEMBERSHIP (STANDARD 14)

The guardian has responsibility to work within agreed objectives, policies standards and procedures of the service as approved by the panel committee.

Appendix III: Case law relating to the role of the guardian

The case law outlined below relates specifically to the role of the guardian ad litem and follows the chapter headings of this book. The general principles derived from case law are set out as a guide. The case law commented on reflects the position as at February 1998. In all circumstances where issues of a legal nature arise the guardian ad litem should seek legal advice from the solicitor.

1. THE DUTIES AND ROLE OF THE GUARDIAN AD LITEM IN SPECIFIED PROCEEDINGS

THE IMPORTANCE OF THE INDEPENDENCE OF THE GUARDIAN AD LITEM
R v Cornwall County Council Ex Parte G (1992) 1 FLR 270.
The local authority (which set up and administered the Panel of guardians ad litem) sought to limit the number of hours which the guardians spent on cases. This was successfully challenged by the guardians. The court commented on the importance of the independence of the guardians and that no restrictions should be imposed on them in the carrying out of their duties; the independence of the guardian ad litem was vital both in terms of the public's confidence in the system and in the guardian's own mind so that the guardian may feel confident of her independent status.

2.THE GUARDIAN AD LITEM AS INVESTIGATOR AND FACT FINDER

I) THE GUARDIAN'S ACCESS TO INFORMATION
The guardian ad litem is entitled to access to certain records held in relation to the child compiled or held by

the local authority. Section 42 Children Act 1989. This would not include the right of access to documents such as police statements or documents from the Crown Prosecution Service. *Nottinghamshire County Council v H (1995) 1 FLR 115*. However, the guardian could apply to the court for access to such documents.

The right of access to local authority records includes access to information compiled by the local authority in its function as an adoption agency and therefore allows the guardian access to confidential adoption records in relation to that child. *Re. T (A minor) (Guardian ad Litem: Case Record) (1994) 1 FLR 632*.

Where the local authority records reveal information which the guardian considers relevant but the local authority state they do not intend to disclose the guardian should raise such matters with the court. Where the local authority raises public interest immunity the guardian cannot disclose the information without the court's agreement. *Re: C (Expert Evidence: Disclosure: Practice) (1995) 1 FLR 204*

II) RESTRICTIONS ON THE GUARDIAN'S USE OF INFORMATION

The guardian can inform other parties of information obtained during the course of his enquiries which is relevant to the case. However, disclosure of information to other agencies such as the police requires leave of the court.

In *Oxfordshire County Council v P (1995) 1FLR 552* the mother made admissions to the guardian that she had injured her child. The guardian passed the information to the social worker. The social worker passed it to the police. The police contacted the guardian and prepared a statement from her. The court held that the passing of information relating to the proceedings between parties did not breach the rules of confidentiality. Accordingly the passing of the information to the social worker was acceptable. However, the guardian should not have made a statement for the police without the court's permission. The court also commented on the fact that the social worker should be able to tell the police but that without the leave of court the police use of such information should be limited.

In *Re. G (Social Worker: Disclosure) (1996) 1FLR 276*
the court said that a social worker could tell the police of
the admission made by the parent to the social worker.
However, this does not appear to have altered the position
vis à vis guardians – the court went on to say that the
position of the guardian and social worker are different,
social workers having duties beyond the proceedings and
guardians being confined to proceedings. The court was
not prepared to comment on what the position would be
had the admission by the parent come via the guardian,
nor the position of the guardian in relation to disclosure
to police, since this was not a matter before the court in
this case.

3. THE GUARDIAN AD LITEM AS CASE MANAGER

THE CO-ORDINATION OF EXPERTS

*Re. C (Expert Evidence: Disclosure: Practice) (1995) 1FLR
749.* Care proceedings often involve a large number of
experts and it is important that the areas of agreement and
disagreement are identified in advance of any hearing. The
co-ordination of the experts is often a matter best
managed by the guardian (or by the local authority).

4. THE GUARDIAN AD LITEM AND THE CHILD

I) PROMISES OF CONFIDENTIALITY

The guardian should not promise to the child that
information given by the child will be withheld. However,
the guardian could tell the child that the judge would be
told that the child did not want the information disclosed
and why, and the guardian can ask the court to determine
whether the information should be disclosed and if so
how. *Re C (Disclosure) (1996)1 FLR 797*

II) CONFLICT BETWEEN CHILDREN THE SUBJECTS OF PROCEEDINGS.

Where a guardian is appointed to represent more than one
child in proceedings and the interests of those children
conflict there is no reason why the guardian cannot
properly represent all the children involved. This does of
course assume that one or more of the children do not
have the requisite capacity to instruct their solicitor

directly. In *Re. T and E (Proceedings: Conflicting Interests) (1995) 1 FLR 581* the guardian identified and defined the interests of each child, conducted a balancing exercise between the interests of each child and gave the court of her view of where the balance fell. This process was approved by the court.

III) THE CHILD'S CAPACITY TO INSTRUCT THE SOLICITOR

The guardian must be alert from the outset that there may be a conflict between what the guardian believes to be in the interests of the child and the child's wishes especially where the child may have capacity to instruct the solicitor directly. *Re. M (Care Proceeding: Child's Wishes) (1994) 1 FLR 749*. The court stressed the need for the guardian to address the situation promptly, for the guardian to discuss the subject with the solicitor and to arrange for the issue to be resolved promptly within the court process.

In cases where there is a possibility of the child instructing the solicitor but a question as to whether the child's emotional disturbance is so intense as to destroy his capacity to instruct then it would be appropriate to seek the advice of any expert already involved in the case. *Re. H (A Minor) (Care Proceedings) (1993) 1 FLR 440*.

5. THE GUARDIAN AD LITEM AND ADOPTION

CONFIDENTIALITY OF REPORTS

The Adoption Rules 1984 provide that the guardian's report is confidential and cannot be disclosed to the parties without permission of the court. In *Re. D (Minors) (Adoption Reports: Confidentiality) (1995) 2 FLR 687* the court set out the test to be applied by the court in determining whether to order disclosure of information in a report to a party. The test to be applied seeks to protect the interests of the child whilst balancing that against the principle of fairness to a party namely that a party is generally entitled to know the information taken into account by the court. The court may therefore order disclosure of some or all of the guardian's report to the parties.

6. THE GUARDIAN AD LITEM AND THE LEGAL SYSTEM

I) THE END OF THE GUARDIAN'S ROLE IN PROCEEDINGS.

The guardian's role ends when the proceedings are over. *Kent County Council V C (1993) 1 FLR 308.* The court made a final care order and then directed that the guardian remain involved for 3 months in an advisory capacity. Held by the court that upon the final decision of the court neither the court nor the guardian had an ongoing function.

Where the court makes a direction under section 37 Children Act 1989 and has made or is considering whether to make an interim care order the court must appoint a guardian for the child unless satisfied it is not necessary to do so in order to safeguard his interests. If upon completion of the local authority's enquiries and report to the court the local authority states that it does not intend to commence specified proceedings then the guardian's appointment under section 41 comes an end. In *Re. CE (1995) 1 FLR 26* the court considered how a guardian could continue to be involved in the private law proceedings. See below under notes on the guardian ad litem and other proceedings.

II) THE GUARDIAN'S VIEWS AS EXPRESSED TO THE COURT

The guardian in complying with her duty to the court to comment on the options available to the court will inevitably consider the evidence available. However, during the course of evidence and in the report, the guardian should be careful to recognise that the weighing up of evidence and reaching decisions on disputed facts is a matter for the court. Furthermore the guardian should not express a view on matters outside her expertise. *B v B (Child Abuse: Contact) (1994) 2 FLR 713*

See also *Re. N (Child Abuse: Evidence) (1996) 2 FLR 214* where the court was concerned that the guardian had expressed opinions ranging over areas of child psychology which were beyond the scope of his expertise.

III) WHERE THE COURT DEPARTS FROM THE GUARDIAN'S RECOMMENDATION

Where the guardian's recommendation is departed from by the court the court must justify this by giving reasons. *Re. W (A Minor) (Secure Accommodation Order) (1993) 1 FLR 692*

7. THE GUARDIAN AD LITEM AND REPORT WRITING

CONFIDENTIALITY OF THE GUARDIAN'S REPORT

The court sets out the persons to whom the report may be disclosed. Disclosure beyond such persons is a matter for the court to decide, even after the proceedings are over. In *Re. C (Guardian ad Litem: Disclosure of Report) (1996) 1 FLR 61* the local authority wanted to disclose the guardian's report to the family centre which proposed to provide assistance to the family post care order. The court held that this required permission of the court. Note that the family centre was in fact part of the Social Services Department. Consideration should therefore be given at the final hearing as to whether the guardian's report should be disclosed to other units, agencies or carers. Also whether expert reports obtained by the guardian should be disclosed.

8. THE GUARDIAN AD LITEM AND OTHER PROCEEDINGS

THE GUARDIAN IN PRIVATE LAW PROCEEDINGS

There are no powers in the Family Proceedings Court (Magistrate's court level) to appoint a guardian for the child in private law proceedings. *Essex County Council v B (1993) 1 FLR 866*. There is a power to appoint a guardian in private law proceedings in the County Court and in the High Court but there are potential difficulties regarding funding and the guardian's role. *Re. CE (Section 37 Direction) (1995) 1 FLR 26*

Appendix IV:
Acts, statutes, guidelines and regulations

ACTS
- The Children Act 1989
- The Adoption Act 1976
- The Human Fertilisation and Embryology Act
- The Family Law Reform Act Part IV

REGULATIONS AND RULES
- The Adoption Agencies Regulation 1983
- The Adoption Rules 1984
- Family Proceedings Rules 1991
- Family Proceedings Courts (Children Act 1989) Rules 1991
- The Children Act Allocation Proceedings Order 1991
- The Guardian ad litem and Reporting Officers (Panels) Regulations 1991
- Children (Secure Accommodation) Regulations 1991
- Foster Placement (Children) Regulations 1991
- Placements of Children with Parents Regulation 1991
- Contact with Children Regulations 1991
- Review of Children's Cases Regulations 1991

FROM THE DEPARTMENT OF HEALTH
- Adoption of Children from Overseas 1991
- Hague Conference on Private International Laws 1993
- The Children Act 1989 Guidance and Regulations
  Volume 1 : Court Orders;
  Volume 2 : Family Support, Day Care and Educational Provision;
  Volume 3 : Family Placements;
  Volume 4 : Residential Care;
  Volume 5 : Independent Schools;
  Volume 6 : Children with Disabilities;
  Volume 7 : Guardians ad Litem and Court Related Matters;
  Volume 8 : Private Fostering;
  Volume 9 : Adoption Issues

- Manual of Practice Guidance for Guardians ad litem and Reporting Officers 1992
- A Guide for Guardians ad litem in Public Law Proceedings under CA 1989
- National Standards for Guardians ad litem and Reporting Officers 1995
- Implementing National Standards 1997
- Reporting to Court under the Children Act (HMSO 1996)
- Messages from Research 1995
- The Challenge of Partnership in Child Protection Practice Guide (HMSO 1995)
- Protecting Children – A Guide for Social Workers Undertaking a Comprehensive Assessment (HMSO 1988)

Bibliography

CHILD PROTECTION

Working Together: A guide to arrangements for inter-agency co-operation & the protection of children from abuse. HMSO 1991.

The Challenge of Partnership in Child Protection: Practice Guide SSI 1994

The Memorandum of Good Practice on Video Interviewing of Child Witnesses Home Office and DOH 1992

Protecting Children: a guide for social workers undertaking a comprehensive assessment HMSO 1988.

Significant Harm: Its management and outcome Eds. Adcock, White, Hollows. Significant Publications 1991.

"HOW TO DO IT" BOOKS

Manual of Practice for Guardians ad Litem and Reporting Officers Judith Timms. HMSO 1992.

A guide for Guardians ad Litem in Public Law Proceedings under the Children Act 1989 Stephen Pizzey and Jeff Davis. HMSO 1995.

On Behalf of the Child Anna Kerr, Freda Hudson, Susan Howard & Eva Gregory. Venture Press 1990.

The Guardian ad Litem Pat Munro and Lis Forrester. Jordan 1994.

Time for me: Communicating with Children Suzette Waterhouse. 1987. Available from 34, Bell Lane, Byfield, Northants.

Code of Ethics for Guardians ad Litem and Reporting Officers NAGALRO 1991, revised 1993.

Reporting to the Court under the Children Act Joyce Plotnikoff and Richard Wolfson. DOH 1996.

Implementing National Standards: A guide through quality assurance for the guardian service. DOH 1997.

INQUIRY REPORTS

The Report of the Inquiry into Child Abuse in Cleveland
HMSO 1987.

A Child in Trust: Report of the inquiry into the death of
Jasmine Beckford. London Borough of Brent 1987.

A Child in Mind: Report of the inquiry into the
circumstances surrounding the death of Kimberley Carlile.
London Borough of Greenwich 1987.

The Pindown Experience and the Protection of Children:
The report of the Staffordshire child care inquiry, 1990.
Staffordshire County Council 1991.

RESEARCH

(The first three collections summarise the findings of several
longer studies)

Social Work Decisions in Child Care: Recent Research
Findings and their implications. HMSO 1985.

Patterns and Outcomes in Child Placement: Messages from
current research and their implications. HMSO 1991.

Child Protection: Messages from Research. HMSO 1995.

Inter-Agency Co-Ordination in Child Protection – Christine
Hallett. HMSO 1995.

*Child Protection Proactive: private risks and public
remedies* – Elaine Farmer and Morag Owen. HMSO 1994.

A Bibliography of Family Placements Literature – Martin
Shaw. BAFF 1994.

RESEARCH FROM FAMILY RIGHTS GROUP

On the Receiving End: Families' experience of the court
process in care and supervision proceedings under the
Children Act 1989. FRG 1994.

RESEARCH FROM DARTINGTON SOCIAL RESEARCH UNIT

Going Home Bullock, Milham and Little. Dartmouth 1993.

Access Disputes in Child Care Milham, Bullock, Hosie and Little. Gower 1989.

ATTACHMENT AND SEPARATION

Clinical Implications of Attachment Concepts Retrospect and Prospect Michael Rutter. Journal of Child Psychology & Psychiatry Vol. 36. No.4 . May 1885.pp549-569. (Review & evaluation of the literature & research; bibliography)

The Emotional Needs of Young Children and their Families: Using Psychoanalytic Ideas in the Community. Eds. Judith Trowell and Marion Bower. Routledge 1996.

WORK WITH BLACK CHILDREN

Social Work with Black Children and their Families Eds., Ahmed, S., Cheetham, J., Small, J. Batsford 1986.

Black, White or Mixed Race? Barbara Tizzard and A. Phoenix. Routledge 1993.

Black Like Me (Workbook One Black Identity; Workbook Two Black Pioneers; Workbook Three Mixed Parentage) Jocelyn E. Maxime. Available from Emani Publications, 125, Avenue Road, Beckenham, Kent, BR43 4RX.

Ethnicity and Child Care Placements Peter M. Smith and David Berridge. NCB.

LOCAL AUTHORITY

The Care of Children Principles and practice in regulations and guidance. HMSO 1990.

Looking after Children: assessing outcomes in child care HMSO 1990.

Perspectives in Child Care Policy Lorraine Fox Harding. Longman 1991.

PERIODICALS AND JOURNALS

Representing Children Quarterly. IRCHIN/NAGALRO.

Family Law Monthly Jordans.

Adoption and Fostering Quarterly. BAAF.

Child Right Children's Legal Centre.

Seen and Heard Quarterly. NAGALRO.

Clinical Child Psychology & Psychiatry Quarterly. Sage Publications.

HUMAN FERTILISATION AND EMBRYOLOGY

Surrogacy, a Guide for Guardians ad Litem in applications for Section 30 orders, The Human Fertilisation and Embryology Act Blythe, E., Richards, J. & Timms, J. IRCHIN 1995.

Birth Power, the Case for Surrogacy Shale, C. Yale University Press, 1989.

Children's Welfare, Surrogacy & Social Work Blyth, F. British Journal of Social Work, 1994, 23, pp259-275.

Surrogacy Ethical Considerations British Medical Association Occasional Paper Ethics No. 1, August 1990.

Other titles available in the Practitioner's Guide series

VENTURE PRESS

VENTURE PRESS

Dealing with Aggression   *Brian Littlechild*

How can aggression and violence to staff in social work and social care settings be managed? This book sets out in a clear and concise manner an integrated approach to the wide range of problems presented by aggression and violence. It covers risk assessment and coping strategies from the perspectives of the different individuals involved, and of staff groups and agencies. The best strategies for dealing with aggression face to face are presented, as are ways we can most effectively reduce risk. For students and experienced workers alike, this book gives a comprehensive account of how to increase safety at work.

ISBN: 1.873878 98 2

Down's Syndrome and Dementia   *Diana Kerr*

This book defines good practice in needs assessment and the provision of services for the growing number of people with Down's Syndrome and Dementia. It is based on a social model which demands that we see the person first and the disease second. It gives many practical examples of ways in which workers and carers can intervene to support people and avoid behaviour and practices which disempower and can harm. It will be relevant to social workers, social care workers, community nurses, carers, staff in supported accommodation and anyone working in community settings.

ISBN: 1.86178 017 6

Drugs, Children and Families   *Jane Mounteney & Harry Shapiro*

This book aims to demystify the drug phenomenon, and increase social workers' knowledge of drug use, by providing a range of up-to-date information about drugs and their effects, by exploring ways drug use may arise as an issue for clients and social services departments and through exploration of a range of social work interventions. *Drugs, Children and Families* draws on relevant research where this exists and highlights a number of concerns, particularly in relation to interventions and provision for young people with drug use problems.

ISBN: 1 86178 013 3

The Art of Assessment   *Laura Middleton*

Good assessment is fundamental to good practice; for all potential service users regardless of age. It is an analytical process that requires intelligence, logic, flexibility, open-mindedness and creativity, and it should be experienced by the consumer as a positive contribution to their life. But it is more complicated than that. No assessment occurs in isolation, but within a competitive and often hostile environment which has to be understood and managed. This book offers a rough guide to this changing and imperfect world, and suggests a model for a value-based assessment within it.

ISBN: 1 873878 87 7

Challenging Local Authority Decisions   *Ann McDonald*

This book examines how dissatisfaction with outcomes can be used positively to challenge local authority decisions. Sometimes it will be the service provision that is challenged; at other times, it will be the way in which that decision is reached and the procedures used which are considered oppressive or unfair. All practitioners should know how to challenge local authority decisions through use of complaints procedures; default powers; referrals to the Ombudsman; or through the courts. In doing so good practice is reinforced, legality is tested and rights upheld.

ISBN: 1 86178 015 X

Deafness and the Hearing *Jennifer Harris*

This book invites a radical change in the majority view on Deafness. The author spent four years studying an organisation of Deaf people in the UK and analysing the reactions of the Hearing majority. The results were dramatic; descriptions of stigmatism, oppressive practice and prejudicial attitudes emerged. The message of the book is that it is not deafness itself which determines social exclusion but entrenched prejudicial attitudes of 'the Hearing'.

ISBN: 1 86178 016 8

Community Care: Working in Partnership with Service Users *Jenny Morris*

This book sets out four principles for working in partnership with people who need support in their daily lives: entitlement; the social model for disability; needs-led assessment; and promoting choice and control. Drawing on the wealth of research and information now available about how to work in ways which empower people. Examples are given relating to all the community care service user groups – older people, people with learning difficulties, those with physical/sensory impairment and people who use mental health services.

ISBN: 1 873878 91 5

Working with Visually Impaired People: Bridging Theory and Practice
Sally French, Maureen Gillman & John Swain

This guide has been written from the experience of visually disabled people and the growing voice of the Disabled People's Movement. The authors take a civil rights perspective to visual disability, which is underpinned by the social model of disability. Two of the authors are themselves visually disabled. Working with visually disabled people draws on the discipline of disability studies to guide practitioners who seek to assist visually disabled people to fulfil the lifestyles of their choice.

ISBN: 1 86178 014 0

Dilemmas of Financial Assessment *Greta Bradley & Jill Manthorpe*

The implementation of the NHS and Community Care Act 1990 has impacted on the lives of service users and social workers. This book explores one important area of change: the increasing emphasis on assessing users' financial circumstances in order to maximise their incomes but also to establish their ability to pay for services. For many social workers this is new ground. Some experienced social workers feel anxious and torn between the new culture of community care and the values they associate with traditional social work tasks.

ISBN: 1 873878 90 7

PLUS   **Poverty** *Monica Dowling*

ISBN: 1 86178 025 7

Confronting Disabling Barriers: towards making organisations accessible
John Swain, Maureen Gillman & Sally French

ISBN: 1 86178 027 3

Family Support *Ruth Gardner*

ISBN: 1 86178 026 5

Social Work and HIV/AIDS *Riva Miller & Derval Murray*

ISBN: 1 86178 029 X

To order any of the above titles, or to be kept informed of forthcoming titles in the series, please contact: *Venture Press, British Association of Social Workers, 16 Kent Street, Birmingham B5 6RD. Telephone: 0121 622 4860 Fax: 0121 622 4860*